COME! LET'S JOURNEY TOGETHER

Coffee Table

Tidbits, Tales and Testimonies

Charles T. Clauser

2017

Published by Dad Giuseppi Publishing,
3316 N. Heritage, Springfield MO 65803.

Printed by CreateSpace, an Amazon.com Company.
Printed in the United States of America.

ISBN-10: 0-692-93901-6

ISBN-13: 978-0-692-93901-7

DEDICATION

M ANY FRIENDS AND ASSOCIATES world-wide energized the author over the years by their consistent prayer. Several individuals as concerned prayer warriors and intercessors inspired the writer in his periods of trying times. Some of these dedicated persons identified themselves, others remain known only by God. To all these godly souls, I say, "Thank you," for your love and involvement in our lives and ministries.

As you read, story after story herein, may you sense the guiding hand of the Lord in myriad ways. May these essays and poems bless you.

I also wish to thank Jim Cole-Rous and Rob Sorbo for their assistance in preparing the manuscript.

I give incalculable credit to my dear wife, Mary, for her day-in, day-out prayer. Thank you, Sweetheart!

Charles

INTRODUCTION

P EOPLE LOVE TO READ and hear stories that lift their spirits and inspire their outlook on life. Reflection and insight cause them to laugh,
cry a lot, even grasp for a moral principle which may reside in their soul for
a lifetime.

Come! Let's Journey Together contains a variety of coffee table
essays, some memoirs, a few unusual experiences, including both fiction and
non-fiction heart-warming events. Most essays were written within the last
thirty years. This compendium of easy-read stories includes devotional
thoughts and a smattering of poetical forms in common usage.

The sections have been divided into Christmas highlights, morality
issues, unusual life experiences, life seen through a poetic lens, and stories
written for friends with a bit of buffoonery added in. I started writing short
stories and poetry during our time as missionaries in the Philippines.

I love the depth and scope of the written word. It may present a
lesson for daily living, or teach about the world around us, or cause us to
delve into the purpose of life.

After savoring the well-spiced meat of *Come! Let's Journey Together*, it is the author's hope the reader will feel blessed in spirit, strengthened in his life activities, and encouraged in his interpersonal relationships with other people.

TABLE OF CONTENTS

I. CHERISHED CHRISTMAS CELEBRATIONS

1. A CHRISTMAS DILEMMA

Non-Fiction:
(1959)

BILLOWS OF BLACK GOO gushed out the backside of the right engine fifteen minutes after take-off from the London military air base. I looked out the window—dumb-founded. We six U.S enlisted guys expected to return on this free hop back to Stuttgart, Germany before our 1959 Christmas passes expired.

With this sudden discovery, I beckoned to one of the DC-3 pilots and said, "The right engine sprung a leak. It's shooting out oil." He took one quick look out my window, then strode quickly to the cockpit for a conference with the pilot-in-charge.

We felt an immediate 180-degree change of direction, the crew up front intent on a safe return to our point of departure.

The only thing I could see through my smeared window—the choppy English Channel, 4,000 feet below. Not a boat in sight as we flew along with one engine, the crippled motor turned off.

We six passengers expressed consternation to each other and hoped the dead, but overheated engine would not catch fire, or explode due to gas leaks and loss of oil.

I tried to look ahead and assess my personal situation in this unexpected turn of events. I knew that if the pilots could not find mechanics to repair the ruptured oil line within the next two days, my personal return to Stuttgart would become a difficult task.

My mind tried to process the fact that if I did not report in to my unit in two days, I would be considered Absent-With-Out-Leave (A.W.O.L.). A cold sweat began to creep up my back.

I did not wish to spend time in the base clink. My time in lockup might extend my active duty commitment of two years to include more days, maybe weeks of extension.

As I looked down at the turbulent water, I found myself questioning how I might survive a splash in the ocean with the three books I had purchased day before yesterday in a London bookstore. If we had to ditch and swim back to the English countryside, I wondered which book should I try to save?

I can't manage all three. Each book measured at least two inches in thickness. The combination of all three had become a heavy load to pack around.

I tried to decide, shall I hold on to my *Tibetan Book of the Dead*, or my *Egyptian Book of the Dead*, or my 2 ½-inch thick book about metaphysics? I paid a significant amount for those books. My corporal's salary did not allow for extravagant purchases.

This flight emergency, a disconcerting dilemma, grew bigger in my mind with each passing minute. What caused this sabotage of my Christmas leave plans? Did a mechanic forget to tighten an oil line connection?

I had planned well in order to receive time off from my assignment of playing assistant first French horn in the Seventh U.S. Army Symphony and I looked forward to my visit to London that I might meet my fiancé's pen-pal and her husband, June and Roy.

Her family welcomed me beyond my expectations after I showed them her picture as my identification and explained my reason for being on leave in England. They even gave me a tour of some well-known London tourist sites, such as the London Bridge and Westminster Abbey. I also had the privilege of sampling their excellent English cooking and Christmas pastries.

But now, indecision. Could this crippled plane make it back to the air base with the loss of Engine Number Two? Or would we have to ditch and endure an unwelcome dunk in freezing waters? After listening for several minutes to the labored drone of the stressed Number One Engine, the pilot made a successful landing. We all breathed normally again.

The pilots talked with the mechanics while we waited for a report. The announcement: "Be ready to fly tomorrow morning at 10:00 a.m., providing the weather cooperates for our safe return to the mainland."

What they meant, but didn't say, "if no heavy fog accumulates overnight that might cause icing on the wings." London, I knew, could be cold at this time of year and harbor a bitter wind chill.

Well, what to do and where to spend the night? I was not allowed to billet overnight at the air base since I was not a visiting officer. So, I returned to the U.S. Servicemen's Center for overnight accommodations where I had stayed for the two previous nights.

Then I went back to visit that kind family again, with whom my wife had been corresponding since age eleven. Although quite surprised, they invited me into their home for the second time.

I must have said the right things and acted somewhat intelligently. Because in 1987, my wife and I spent a week with those dear people while on a return trip from the U.S. to the Philippines for our second missionary term with the Assemblies of God.

I did not know the Lord Jesus personally until February 15, 1973. But unbeknown to me, the Lord took care of me in marvelous ways throughout my earlier years, as on this trip. We did fly out the next day and I did return to my unit before my Christmas pass expired. Praise the Lord! No A.W.O.L.

Jesus gave me a wonderful Christmas celebration in London that year. Now, for over 65 years, my wife and her English pen-pal have continued to correspond by letter and more recently by e-mail

I must add, I later burned the two books about "the Dead" and disposed of the metaphysical book, too. But that's a story for another time. Perhaps someday over lunch, complete with a cup of hot English tea!

2. CHRISTMAS FRUITCAKE

(1997)

I LOVE FRUITCAKE. And, I believe fruitcake should be authorized and supported in every state of our United States of America as the national fruit and cake dessert.

Uh . . . Men, did you hear the ladies groan?!

I believe fruitcake should be sold tax free, packaged in metal containers, with either three-, five-, or ten-pound capacities, sealed, wrapped with a red ribbon, and a green bow. Priced low, so children might buy this delicious and tasty pastry year-round, especially at Christmas time. Young people ought to be allowed by their parents, the pleasure of sharing such a delicacy with friends and family members.

To illustrate my feelings, I want to relate a story about understanding the importance of fruitcake. During one of our missionary itineration years, Mary and I spoke throughout the months of January and early February about the significance of Valentine's Day.

We, of course, emphasized God's *agape* love. Another theme in those services emphasized what gifts a husband might give his wife at that time of year as an appropriate token to show his love for her.

Mary and I married on August 13, 1960. As our first February together approached, I tried to decide: "For Valentine's Day, shall I give her a box of Russell Stover chocolates, which I knew she enjoyed?" Or, "Shall I give her a large box of fruitcake, which I savored?"

My mouth salivates every time I think of sinking my teeth into a succulent piece of moist, full-bodied fruitcake. (Excuse me, please, while I swallow.)

Something in the mixture of the fruitcake, including the chopped nuts, the various pieces of candied fruit, the texture of banana bread-like cake, made me lean toward purchasing the best fruitcake I could find.

I delighted, also, in feasting, whenever possible, on a couple of caramel chocolates. The milk chocolates seemed to tempt a person to take just one more piece. In fact, various varieties joined the chorus: "Open me up, take another bite. You may never experience an opportunity like this again."

Oh, dear. What a dilemma. Our first Valentine's Day together, I must make the right decision. Even though we agreed before marriage to never divorce, a mistake in this critical decision might strain our relationship to the breaking point before our first year together passed by.

You probably guessed the result of my difficult decision —yes, fruitcake. But, when I saw the disappointment on Mary's face, I knew I would likely end up in the doghouse for days. A dark cloud of gloom temporarily dampened the atmosphere inside our home.

I learned a lesson that day in "smooth interpersonal relationships" (S-I-R, for you missionary inclined people). On Valentine's Day the next year, I presented my wife a big, two-layered box of chocolates, the kind with several assorted pieces.

The look on her face told me I had made the right choice. She wrapped her arms around me, gave me a big hug, and a kiss that dispelled any remembrance of my previous year's *faux pas*. Yes, I learned my lesson about fruitcake, and that most of the time, my wife's cravings for certain kinds of sweets take precedence over my desires.

At this point in our missionary services, after relating this incident, I always asked: "If given a choice for either chocolates or fruitcake, how many people in the congregation would prefer to receive fruitcake for Valentine's Day?" Almost all the men would raise their hands—few, if any women.

Then I asked: "Similarly, how many persons in the congregation would prefer instead, to receive a box of chocolates for Valentine's Day?" Almost every woman would raise a hand —few, if any men. The result surprised me: the women overwhelmingly preferred chocolates; the men evidenced a passion for fruitcake, with little or no cross-over.

Please allow me to conduct this same survey today. "Dear Reader, if given a choice for chocolates or for fruitcake, would you prefer to receive a box of chocolates for Valentine's Day in the coming year?" Or even today? Or for this Christmas?"

Please raise your hands -- high . . . .

Okay. Thank you.

"Similarly, how many hands for fruitcake?

Ooh, I think I know the answer . . . need I ever again, ask such a silly question?

Merry Christmas, friends! And, may God bless you in the coming New Year!

3. CHRISTMAS WITH JOSE

(1947)

MY FAMILY CELEBRATED Christmas Eve 1947 after Dad and I hand-milked three cows, fed them, provided fresh straw for their beds in the barn, and shoveled clean the area behind each animal. The farm chores included milk placed in a large pan for three kittens, slop for a mother pig, and warmed-up hash for Jose, our Great Pyrenees, 50-pound, ten-month old sheep dog.

Uncle Don in Santa Fe, NM, told Dad: "If you will pay the railroad freight on Jose, I'll send him up to you." Little did Dad know, the six-month old pup would weigh 40 pounds and cost $47.50 for the expensive freight charges up to Ontario, OR, the closest railroad stop near our home in Payette, ID.

Jose arrived in August after a three-day train ride, stiff and barely able to move because of the tight quarters of his wooden, radio-crate cage, 24-inches wide, 48-inches long, and 30-inches high, with one triangular wire-mesh opening, approximately 10 inches on each side. That end served as a door for the crate. While en route, Jose chewed through the wire mesh in an effort to escape.

The freight employee feed and watered Jose once a day throughout his journey. Upon Jose's arrival, Dad placed the crate with dog inside, on the back of our pick-up truck. When Dad opened the crate in our backyard, he had to lift Jose off the back of the truck and set him on the ground. The pup could not walk nor jump down under his own power, because of stiffness in his legs incurred while on the train ride.

At home, Dad told my sister and me: "We'll leave Jose tied up. Wait three days before you pet and play with him. By that time, he will start to become acquainted with you."

It happened as Dad indicated. The dog accepted all of us as friends after that initial orientation and waiting period.

I learned basic carpentry skills in my teen years from Dad, who, at one time, worked as a finished cabinetry carpenter. At my age 13, he helped me build a dog house for Jose that looked somewhat like a human's house, but in miniature, with dimensions four feet wide, six feet long, three feet high, with peaked roof, and double walls and roof, all filled with sawdust insulation purchased from the local sawmill.

Jose had everything in that house except electricity and water connections. I think he enjoyed his new home. After I completed the paint job, I knew all family members expressed pride in the finished product.

Highway 30 North, a major north/south artery, located in front of our home, abounded with traffic. One summer, Jose, not yet streetwise, ran into a car, broke a leg, and dragged himself somehow up to my grandpa's apple orchard, 100 yards away from our home.

Grandpa George found him the next day, took his work horse Tommy and the stone boat (a sled with flat top, six feet square, used for carrying rocks out of a field), and brought Jose back to us.

Jose seemed repentant and glad to see us again. He later recovered. But throughout the time of our living on this acreage north of Payette, we lost two dogs in similar types of vehicular accidents.

An unusual sight happened one summer when Boss August came to our home with the neighborhood custom combining crew to thrash our five acres of wheat. August made the rounds of all our neighbors who had small acreages of grain ready for the harvest. I remember August as a fine gentleman.

For example, after the noon meal at our house, which had been prepared by all the neighborhood ladies for the twelve-man crew, who came because of their own small harvest needs (3-10 acres), August picked up his dishes and placed his stack in the kitchen sink.

Then he said: "You men pick up your dishes, too, and place them on the counter. These ladies worked hard to prepare this fine meal for us. We must do our part." End of conversation; everyone obeyed without question.

But amid the loud combine noise of an old-fashioned heavy-duty tractor and the antique combine itself, one neighborhood dog decided to challenge Jose's territorial rights, barred his teeth and growled. In a split second, Jose flipped that dog over on its back and placed both his paws on the stomach and chest of the surprised assailant.

Jose looked down at the confused mutt, and growled, ready to go for its jugular vein. Four men separated the two dogs. All other dogs cowered well out of sight of Jose.

Without hesitation, the defeated intruder vacated the premises. The men laughed and felt they had witnessed a better event than a Jack Dempsey boxing match.

One summer day, Jose found a baby chick running loose outside the wire-mesh enclosed chicken pen attached to our garage. He apparently thought, "Let's play!"

So, he picked up the chick in his big slobbery mouth, flipped the chick into the air, and repeated the process a few times. Dad stopped Jose's game of 'come play with me' before Jose could drown the two-week old chick with his saliva.

Jose's all-white coat consisted of at least a one-half inch of matted hair encasing his body, which gave the appearance of a woven rug, itself overlaid with thick two- to three-inch long strands of coarse straight hair.

I remember one winter day, I looked out our back door toward the barn and there lay gentle Jose. He sat panting, curled on top of a new three-inch snowfall.

One of our barnyard cats snuggled into his flank and fell asleep. An extraordinary scene—close friends enjoying each other's company.

But, the rascal! Jose's excessive appetite caused his downfall. He developed the habit of visiting all of our farm neighbors within a one-mile circuit and begging food.

Each neighbor found him unique, offered him a snack, and gave him a condescending pat. Or, on his area travels, he would eat whatever appeared in any outside dog dish.

But one morning, a neighbor lady stepped out of her house, wearing her housecoat, not yet fully dressed, walked a few steps to her nearby garden, and began to dig up a couple of potatoes for her family's breakfast menu.

As she bent over to engage in this part of her breakfast preparation, Jose came up behind her and playfully pushed her over into the snow. She managed to stand up, sputtered, not happy. Dad soon knew of her displeasure.

After this incident, Dad realized 80-pound Jose needed a new home. A veterinarian who lived 35 miles away agreed to relocate our canine bum to his farm property.

But Jose developed the same roaming habit at his new residence. We learned he grew heavier, like a butterball, and in a few years died from overweight.

After he died, I remembered how our family celebrated Christmas Eve 1947, our first Christmas with Jose, like the addition of a new child in a young couple's home. Jose remained tethered by a 15-foot chain near our back door which allowed him access to his special dog house.

Inside our home, Grandpa George and Grandma Mary ate Mom's delicious fried chicken dinner with us before we opened Christmas gifts.

Outside, Jose slurped down an extra-large portion of hot mashed potatoes and gravy embedded with bits of corn, peas, and his own allotment of fried chicken. Inside, we wondered how can Jose best serve our family needs and farm responsibilities.

However, when we heard the chain rattle over the transom to his dog house, we knew Jose retired for the night, ready to dream of playful rabbit encounters or some other such exciting dog-type activity. Perhaps, he allowed entrance afterward to one of the barnyard cats who wished to snuggle up to him for the night and share his cozy home interior.

4. JOSE'S DOGHOUSE

(A Seventh-Grade Memoir, 1947)

DAD," I SAID AS WE refilled the chicken house feeders, "Jose needs a doghouse for protection from the cold, winter nights."

"Bud (Dad always called me Bud.), you helped build our new chicken houses and you learned basic carpentry skills doing it. Would you like to construct a home for him yourself?"

"Sure. Can we make the walls double and fill the middle areas with sawdust, like you did for the chicken houses?"

"Of course, I'll show you how to do it. And, you can fill the double floor and ceiling spaces with sawdust, too. It will make a nice snug home for Jose. When you're ready for the sawdust, we'll go out to the saw mill and fill up the back of the pick-up with that insulation for Jose's new home."

"When completed, may I paint the doghouse?"

"Yes. The paint will cover up ugly-looking spots on the wood, both inside and out. We have enough left-over lumber in the garage from the chicken house construction to do the project. You can use those boards for the doghouse."

"Dad, did you ever think of making a doghouse for Jose when you worked on the chicken houses?"

"Not until nearly the end. Because, I didn't know how much scrap lumber we might gather together."

"Dad, will you help me, please? I want to do a good job —saw boards straight and place nails in the right spots the first time."

"You betcha! When completed, we'll place it near the end of Mom's clothesline. Jose will be able to slide his 15-foot chain on the wire strand from the doghouse to the back door steps. He can easily go to Mom when she places food in his dish."

"You're a good carpenter, Dad. Where did you learn the trade?"

"Your Uncle Joe, one of my half-brothers on the Wells side, lived in Glenn's Ferry, Idaho. I worked with him. It was only about ten miles from our home near Bliss. We boys on the Clauser side of the family grew up there during our grade-school years. Our home, sat on a bluff, overlooking the Snake River."

"Wow! With rattlesnakes and jack rabbits, but with good fishing in the River, huh?"

"Well, we didn't take home any petrified watermelons, you know, big round stones. But we managed to catch some trout and catfish in the river."

"Did you ever catch a real big fish in the Snake River?"

"We three boys, Don, Charley, and myself, occasionally caught a four-to-five foot sturgeon. Our fishing in the river helped Grandma Clauser put food on the table. That's because my dad walked away from home and left us stranded before any of us reached age six."

"So that's why you dropped out of high school in Payette between your junior and senior year. You wanted to help support the family and get Uncle Charley graduated!"

"That's where your Uncle Joe comes in the picture. He gave me a job and trained me to be a "finish" carpenter. That means, I learned to build tight cabinets with good sliding drawers. Not every carpenter can do that kind of work."

"Can we get some boards now," I asked as I closed the feed sack, "before Mom calls us for lunch?"

"Yes, Bud. Start your doghouse by making a 4' X 6' platform upon which you can build the four walls. First, nail two 2' X 6" boards together with spikes."

"Ow!

"What happened?"

"I hit my thumbnail with the hammer."

"You okay?"

"Yes, probably later. Right now my thumb throbs."

"Don't work for speed. Start the nail slowly, pound accurately. Keep your eye on the nail head."

"Hello, out there," Mom called as she opened the screen door on the porch and stepped outside. "Dinner will be ready in five minutes. Come wash your hands and face, guys. I'll serve after you sit down at the table. It's fried chicken and mashed potatoes today. Yum, yum!"

"Place your tools together, Bud, out of the sun. If left in the sun, each tool will burn your hand when we return. Let's go wash up, can't keep the cook waiting. Sounds like she made a delicious meal for us."

"I wonder if Mom will serve chocolate cake after dinner with lots of thick cow cream on top. I think her chocolate cake would take out all the pain from my throbbing thumb."

"Let's go find out."

5. HOMEWARD BOUND FOR CHRISTMAS

(1957)

ON SATURDAY<DECEMBER 21, 1957 in Ann Arbor, Michigan, I joined thousands of other University of Michigan students who scattered for the two-week Christmas break.

I boarded the New York Central train at 8:35 a.m. bound for Chicago and transferred to the Union Pacific railway for the ride to Ontario, Oregon, the nearest stop for my hometown, Payette, Idaho, five miles away.

Colorful decorations draped on sidewalk city light poles dulled my Christmas spirit as I rode in a taxi minutes earlier to the railroad station. After the train completed boarding passengers, it seemed to me time remained frozen. We did not move forward one inch for a period of time.

I sighed, settled back in my cushioned chair, and day dreamed of the student nurse I met four weeks earlier on a blind date. I had telephoned her, and we agreed to a hot chocolate encounter, just to satisfy the pesky persistence of two mutual friends—a fellow University of Michigan bandsman and the girl he dated from her dorm.

I already missed the presence of this attractive young lady. For we had continued the habit of a hot chocolate date each day since meeting each other six weeks earlier.

Soon the train sped through the bleak, Michigan winter countryside. I recovered from my gloom to enjoy scenes of snow-covered, barren fields which earlier produced great surpluses of wheat, potato, and corn crops.

But, I found it difficult to set aside my thoughts of student nurse Mary. My mind jumped from dreaming about this new friendship and expecting a joyful reunion with Mom and Dad in central Idaho after the completion of this two day journey.

On the trip west, I wrote three letters each day to Mary. However, I didn't want to overdo a good thing nor risk termination of our friendship, Because, this activity became the best way to get rid of my despondency and live through the monotony of this cross-country, 2,000 mile railroad trek.

The rides both ways caused boredom for passengers who traveled long distances. My solution: sit and read a book, or stand and walk down the aisle, or climb the stairs of the dome liner to exercise my leg muscles and catch a view of corn fields and endless prairie land, or walk to the dining car for another cup of coffee and a cookie, or sleep in my chair and wait for a change of scenery.

Throughout this trip west, I contemplated my future. The first issue: complete the requirements for a master of music degree on brass instruments, with graduation scheduled for January 1958. Next, prepare for the draft notice to appear soon in my mail box and my expected two-year US Army tour of duty.

Then, consider long-range plans to obtain a high school or college band job after my service career. Above all, keep in communication with Mary every day, because marriage might be possible for us in the summer of 1960, if she agrees.

Train travel in the various towns ran through the worst sections of each city as one might judge from the condition of old buildings and dingy surroundings, except for Battle Creek, MI. Its appearance by train looked clean and well-kept.

My Uncle Walt told me later, the influence of the Kellogg cereal owners prompted the beautification of the unglamorous part of this town in order to better promote their products.

The bumpy, sideways motion of the New York Central Line caused a jerky, uncomfortable ride. Nevertheless, after four hours, we arrived at the terminal station in the windy city. I changed Lines and boarded the UP routed to Portland, through Illinois, Iowa, Nebraska, Colorado, Wyoming, Idaho, and Oregon.

The trip for me covered a period of two days and one night, with the reverse trip scheduled for two nights and one day. I made this roundtrip journey three times while enrolled in the master's level instrumental music program at the U of M, a period of three semesters and one summer school session (Fall 1956 – January 1958).

The conductor allowed passengers to move around on the UP Line, walk through all the coaches, and climb stairs to the dome level of the cars. A dome liner coach provided an upper level, 360-degree view through an all-glass canopy. I thrilled at this possibility of beholding terrific panoramic sights in the sunlight hours and gazing at a vast array of stars at night.

Another feature I enjoyed on the 2,000 mile ride across the American heartland -- a walk to the dining car, where a person might take on nourishment in a plush setting. Its high prices, however, stretched the budget for a student on limited finances.

In Ann Arbor, my food budget averaged a total of $2.40 per day: breakfast -- $.50; lunch -- $.65; dinner -- $1.25. I frequented four low-cost restaurants for meals in order to minimize my food bill.

Home at last, I learned Grandma Mary died ten days before I arrived. Mom and Dad felt it better I not leave school to come home for the funeral, but stay in Ann Arbor and finish my classes and assignments before the Christmas break.

My sister Barbara and her husband Don had purchased a home in Washington, D.C. He could not take time away from his new job with the Bureau of Reclamation. Therefore, Christmas 1957 progressed as a bittersweet family occasion.

One of my 1957 Christmas memories -- we ate dinner with our neighbors, Jerry and Mary DeBord. Mary baked pies commercially for the town bowling alley restaurant as I grew up. After dinner I told her, "Why bake anything else but bread? I love your homemade rolls."

Mary expressed her other talents by participation in various civic projects. For example, in the first week of May at the time of my junior and senior high school years, she organized celebrations of historical pageants and parades for our small community.

Jerry DeBord worked as a building contractor. Near the start of WW II, Dad went with Jerry's carpentry crews in 1942

to the Twin Falls, ID area, to help build a government contain-
ment camp for the Japanese who lived in California, Oregon,
and Washington because of possible espionage or insurgent activities against the U.S.

John and Georgia Baldridge, who lived next door to the
DeBords, invited us also to their home for dinner during my
Christmas break. The Baldridges and my parents often played
bridge together and later golfed together. Weather permitting,
they all golfed 18-27 holes each day.

Dad and Mom taught me to play golf, which at one time
before learning to enjoy the game, he referred to with distaste
as "cow pasture pool."

The Christmas break from college in 1957 refreshed me,
and in the middle of my much needed rest at home, I made time
for writing more letters to Mary.

* * * * *

I returned from my two-year military commitment in
Europe in late February of 1960, and after separation from the
Army at a post near Chicago, I sold my trombone for $150 and
purchased a round-trip railroad ticket for Mary, now a registered nurse, to come with me and visit my parents.

The train ride on this journey westward turned into a
combination of tension and conflict scenes like a serial cowboy
movie. In Iowa, the train's heating units in two dome cars froze,

which caused those passengers to move to other cars, ourselves included. Outside Denver, the train hit a truck with a cow in it.

Next, a passenger experienced an epileptic seizure on the walkway at the end of a car. His dental bridge became stuck in his throat. Mary and I directed foot traffic around him. Meanwhile, the conductor called ahead for a doctor to come on board at the next stop and remove the obstruction.

The doctor performed well; our travel through the Rockies continued. Later, in Kemmerer, WY, with two feet of snow on the ground, the train stopped for three hours because of a derailment ahead of us.

Mary wondered, "What next? Will there be a train robbery? Will Indians ride over the hill and surround us?" I, however, managed to step off the train for a few minutes and call home at an outside pay phone attached to the station wall.

Happy to hear from us, Mom telephoned the Ontario station dispatcher and told him of our dilemma. He had no information about the situation or any idea when we might arrive at our destination.

But after a nine-hour delay, we arrived in Ontario, OR, our end-of-ride stop, ready for a jubilant reunion with Mom and Dad. Was it puppy love for Mary or the real thing? I believe the Lord drew us together over 57 years ago to minister for Him as a team. We married on August 13, 1960 in Marion, MI, in Mary's home church, the United Methodist Church.

6. MEMORABLE MOMENTS WITH FRIENDS

(1985, 2000, 2011)

HOW WOULD A PERSON describe the development of quality time in bonded family relationships at this time of year? For example, my family members live far away in Colorado, Nevada, Idaho, Michigan, Minnesota, New Jersey, and North Carolina.

They scurry around in their towns each yuletide, busy in their own ministry and personal activities. So, my question: "How might Mary and I spend our time best in Springfield, MO in fellowship and service to others this Christmas as we enjoy the blessings of the Lord?"

I recall that over the years as Assembly of God missionaries in the Philippines, we celebrated the birth of Jesus with fellow missionaries, Steve and Linda Long. After Division of Foreign Missions approval, the Clausers in 1980 and the Longs in 1981, found that our paths crossed in parallel assignments throughout the next two decades.

We both lived at times in Metro Manila and served at the King's Garden Children's Home in Bataan. Steve and I preached in the same Luzon churches and chaired school-oriented committees for our missionary fellowship, not to mention the many meals our families consumed together in restaurants and in each other's home.

Early in our careers, Mary and I spent much of our 1985 Christmas break with the Longs, because of the cessation of classes at the Far East Advanced School of Theology, where I taught (later renamed, the Asia Pacific Theological Seminary), and the recess for our children from classes at Faith Academy.

Both institutions located in Metro Manila, allowed us time to travel up to the mountains in northern Luzon. The Longs lived in Baguio City, a pine-covered mountain-top, where the American military had developed a rest and relaxation resort called Camp John Hay. Previously, the Japanese military had converted the base into a detention center during WW II.

Together, we survived several earthquake tremors at their home in that late December period. I remember one earthquake shock broadsided us as we ate dinner. The chandelier began to sway above the table. We heard a rumbling sound to the north, like a freight train, which increased in intensity.

A sudden jolt rocked all of us as the ripple passed through their house and the ground below us. The resultant sound then lessened in intensity as the energy wave passed far south of us. The entire event transpired in less than 30 seconds.

Walter and Lucille Erola, senior A/G missionaries who ministered among the Ilocano tribes of Northern Luzon, attended the dinner party that evening. He related how earlier in the rainy season, he drove back to Baguio on slippery mountain roads in heavy rain from a ministry trip.

Near Baguio, he looked in his rear-view mirror and saw a large portion of a steep hillside, slide down on to the road behind him covering two cars. He immediately thanked God and realized his protection had come as a miracle from the Lord.

Before dinner that evening, I glanced at the shoe and boot rack near the Long's front door. Steve's boots showed signs of a 3/8's-inch thick cluster of mud and mold growth on each sole. Mold grows fast in moist areas in the wet months at Baguio's mile-high altitude.

Therefore, the mountain residents install light bulbs in their clothes closets which produce heat and help prevent the excessive growth of mold. The light bulb treatment maintains dry wardrobes.

Years later, both our families lived in Metro Manila. Whenever the stress of driving in the over-crowded city traffic and breathing the high pollution content of vehicle exhaust exceeded our tolerance and stamina, we telephoned the Longs: "Got a VHS movie, something funny to watch? We need a few good laughs."

Linda would reply: "Sure. Come on over. We can watch a couple of MASH episodes or a movie spoof like "The Gods Must Be Crazy."

At one Christmas celebration in the Long's home, recently arrived from Malaysia, A/G missionaries Berent and Margaret Knutsen, joined the dinner party. However, the discovery of termites in the door frame located between the kitchen and dining room interrupted the festivities for a few minutes.

Needless to say, the holiday banquet proceeded as scheduled. Later, the landlord exterminated the termites and replaced the door frame.

Steve and I ministered together in various ways. For example, we once traveled three hours north from Metro Manila to Zambales and on from the Subic Bay area up the shoreline to a Refugee Resettlement Camp, whose residents survived the June 15, 1991 Mount Pinatubo volcanic activity.

On another ministry trip which resulted from the disastrous Pinatubo eruption, four of us – Steve, Harry, Rick, and I, delivered two freight truckloads of relief food to A/G pastors and families in their congregations at four locations in the devastated farm areas of Central Luzon.

In those years, Mary and Linda served on food and health committees, and attended to missionary health issues (both had pursued nursing careers earlier in their lives).

Both families worked on assignments for a variety of situations such as teaching, music, family responsibilities, missionary fellowship, end-of-month business and social meetings, and new missionary orientation.

During Christmas 2000, Steve and Linda came to our home in Angeles City, central Luzon, site of the former U.S. Clark Air Base for a get-together. Newly arrived MA's (missionary associates) Ken and Melba Drew from Michigan, drove up from Valenzuela City (Site of Bethel Bible College on the northern side of Metro Manila.) to join us.

This overnight visit necessitated Steve and Linda sleeping on our air mattress in the living room. We gave our guest room to Ken and Melba, because they were "the new kids on the block."

At that time, we lived in a subdivision about one mile south of the Angeles City Air Base (Location of a five-story hospital during WW II). I think as many dogs lived in this housing development as people.

Ken and Melba ministered at the King's Garden Children's Home for two years, but lived on the BBC campus in northern Metro Manila, where they took an active part in the campus life.

45

When a person considers the interrelationship between close friends, like the Long/Clauser/Morar association with its links stronger than super glue, what will this connection be like in heaven? Won't we express that same togetherness with everyone we see in heaven?

Jesus said in John 14:2-3: "In my Father's house are many mansions . . . I go to prepare a place for you . . . where I am, there you may be also" (NKJV). It sounds to me like one super-family operation with Holy Spirit anointed affiliations, bonded for eternity.

We will work together, laugh abundantly, enjoy a variety of jokes, swap stories, and above all, endlessly and foremost, praise the Lord.

Both our families now reside in north Springfield, MO. The Longs continue their ministry assignments at Global University.

Mary and I enjoy retirement at Maranatha Village, involved with busy schedules and a multitude of activities. Last Saturday, December 3, 2011 marked Kris' 35th birthday. This Sunday, December 11th, will mark Steve's 63rd birthday.

Tonight, Friday, December 9, 2011, we celebrate also the 86th birthday of Leota Morar. She and husband John served several years in the Philippines, first in Metro Manila at Bethel Bible College and the Far East Advanced School of Theology.

After John died, Leota served in Baguio City at APTS in various capacities, including the office of registrar. The word "precious" best describes our times together with Leota, both in the Philippines and stateside.

I lost count of the number of past Christmases in which with Leota, Steve and Linda, we took pleasure in sharing Christ's love and provision. Together we each shared lots of laughs and happy times as well as periods of sorrows and disappointments.

How much greater and more abundant though, will a person's friendship grow with others when we arrive in heaven? And, at the marriage supper of the Lamb, our love of family, of camaraderie, and of faithfulness to the Lord will connect our hearts with others in greater praise for Jesus, our magnificent Creator.

7. A BIBLE INSTITUTE FOR THE DEAF
CHRISTMAS PARTY

(An adaptation of the December 1998 BID Christmas party events)

THE VALENZUELA CITY TEMPERATURE in Metro Manila, home to the Bible Institute for the Deaf, cooled to 72^0 F. the afternoon of the annual faculty, staff, and student Christmas blow-out (meaning, a gala end-of-semester dinner followed by a program, skits, and parlor games). Next to the graduation day activities, the Christmas dinner party gained great popularity for all campus personnel.

Twelve college classmates, five boys and seven girls, conversed with signs as they arranged decorations along the walls, ceiling, and windows of the BID dining room in preparation for the celebration. The tallest boy, J.V. (Joseph Vicente), signed in desperation to E.C. (Mom Ellen Castillo), "We need more space for our *paroles* and those of the high schoolers.

"We used the entire window space for our own Christmas wreaths. Everyone's art work, however, should receive equal recognition." (The deaf speak to each other by the use of a person's initials, which simplifies their sign language.)

The *parole*, a unique Philippines adornment, exists as a distinctive cultural Christmas decoration, in size as small as a three-inch five-pointed star in a circle, and as large as an eight-foot-in-diameter star secured in a circular frame.

Lighted *paroles,* resemble flashing neon signs and measure two to four feet in diameter. Construction materials consist of wire, paper, tinfoil, *capiz* shells, or colored tissue-thin cellophane. The *parole* may hang on a door knob, drape a window, or occupy a prominent place in the entry way to a home or business.

"Agreed," President E.C. (Mom Ellen Castillo) smiled as she signed in response. "I shall send J.P. (Jessie Poria) to help you make space for each beautiful piece. Please remember to place ribbons, bows, and streamers on the walls."

"Yes Ma'am, and please request Sir Jessie to bring a step ladder. We want to hang our smallest *paroles* and other ornaments from the ceiling," R.A. (Romeo Albay) replied with small signs of appreciation, a look of satisfaction on his face.

Sir Jessie, the custodian, arrived in minutes and motioned to all the boys, "I brought both string and wire to use as we hang your exhibits." Being shorter in stature, he looked at, J.V., "did you and your classmates make a plan for the arrangement of the decorations?"

R.A. stopped his preparations by the front door and signed with a big grin on his face, "Yes, we want to hang the larger *paroles* by the windows and the smallest *paroles* from the ceiling."

"Looks fine," J.V. observed as he positioned the ladder by the kitchen counter. "I believe people can walk around the tables with ease and not bump into any decorations."

"I'll hold the ladder for you, J.V.," custodian J.P. said. "Careful. Don't lean out too far when you work at the top step. No accidents allowed . . . Ah, good boy. Your arrangement gives depth, a nice mix of color, and variety in sizes to the display."

Activities of this kind exist as group events. All persons in the area participate and work together. If not, a single person working by himself will exhibit a sad, lonely face.

A few minutes later Ma'am Ellen returned to the dining room with a bag full of various kinds of chocolate bars, candies, and M + M's. Enroute to the kitchen she stopped and surveyed the busy decorating activity with a discerning eye.

"I like it. What a nice setting to honor King Jesus. We shall play games after dinner and open presents in His honor." (Filipinos dramatize events well at any age and love to play games that require active physical and emotional participation.)

Each student, even each teacher, had found a favorite spot to prepare for the evening. Some girls proceeded to set out the table arrangements of flowers, garlands, plates, silverware, and other miscellaneous items for the festive dinner.

Boys handled the heavy work, often chiding or teasing the girls. For example: "Don't climb the ladder, S.E. (Suzette Enguero), you might fall off." Or, "Be sure to move that box by the front window M.D. (Malou Dacayuman), just a little more to the left. If it rains later this afternoon, those presents may turn into a soggy mess."

The quick-witted girls would banter back with a twinkle in their eyes, "You fear heights, not me." Or, "Did you forget? It does not rain at this time of year."

President Ellen and Sir Jessie stood back for a moment from the organized chaos of the social event. E.C. commented proudly: "The students this year work together better than last year. I think they display more initiative in their desires to complete projects than our group last year.

For example, R.I. (Raymond Ilagan) doesn't wait for a request from us to arrange the chairs in here or stack them to make room for class activities. He looks ahead and sees the need to prepare the table and chair placement for our classes and meal times."

J.P. nodded, "Yes, and did you notice M.S. (Marissa Santiago) walks with her head up. She socializes better this year with the other girls. Her home life, I feel, does little to encourage her language skills."

Three hours later, the decorations glistened with eye-catching reflections from the overhead lights. The crowd began to arrive. Each person commented on the nice table settings, the gift packages, and the P.A. system – all preparations completed.

The food table hot trays and dishes of prepared food sat ready for the dinner activity to commence: bowls of hot, steamy rice (*kanin*), plates of bread rolls (*pandesal*), mixed vegetables (*mga gulay*), eggplant (*talong*), noodles (*pansit*), boiled eggs (*mga itlog*), large dishes of chicken (*manok* and *adobe*), shrimp (*hipon*), fish (*tilapia* and *bangus*), pineapple (*pinya*), cooking bananas (*saba* and *saging*), choice Filipino desserts like coconut (*buko*) pie, and mixed candies (*halo-halo*).

"Ma'am," F.L. (Fely Liwanag), the faithful cook spoke through her perspiration while standing in front of the kitchen stove, "My kitchen crew stands ready by the food tables to serve or assist as needed. Please pray for the Lord's blessing before the food turns cold." Meanwhile, L.S. (Liza Sia) placed the soft drinks and water bottles by each plate.

"Good," E.C. responded. She stood tall as she clapped her hands three times above her head, then spoke and signed: "Attention everyone, I shall ask our assistant chairman of the board, Rev. Pete Tiapson, to ask the Lord's blessing over our dinner and evening together. Brother Pete. . . ."

Some of the staff and students spoke as well as signed, due to an illness or accident earlier in their lives. Others were born deaf.

The delicious banquet showed off F.L.'s fine culinary skills. Laughter, the clanking of silverware, and the sudden disappearance of favorite foods highlighted the first event of the party.

The moderator for the after-dinner program, H.M. (Helen Molina), played her guitar and sang *The Birthday of a King*. S.A. (Sophia Arangote), the BID librarian, read the Christmas story from Luke 2:1-14.

President E.C. led everyone in signing and singing the familiar carol, *It Came Upon the Midnight Clear*, while H.M. accompanied this part of the congregational participation with her guitar.

Games for all, student skits, and the distribution of gifts, continued throughout the next hour, interspersed with more carols and popular Christmas songs, some in Tagalog, the language of the Metro Manila area.

Each month of the school year, a special event, a national holiday, or a birthday became the reason for a joyous get together for students and staff to indulge in a special meal or refreshment. These activities were greeted with anticipation because most students came from homes with few financial resources.

This particular evening glorified Jesus through conversations, singing, fellowship, and laughter. It became a night long remembered. An event with Jesus sitting among us, amid growing friendships, and the sharing His eternal love.

Later, expressions of awe and appreciation over the large portions of Neapolitan ice cream (*sorbetes*) dished up for each person, with even generous second helpings caused eyes to bulge in amazement and thankfulness. Older students told younger ones about the smaller amounts of food served in previous years at this annual BID festivity.

Next, with everyone singing and signing, the high school boys signed *O Come All Ye Faithful*, followed by the high school girls who signed *O Little Town of Bethlehem*. All the high schoolers together signed *Hark the Herald Angels Sing* as a closing song for the evening festivities.

8. *MISSION LEADERS RECEIVE PITH HELMET*
AWARDS

(2001)

YOU KNOW THE TRADITION. A few decades ago, you were not a "real" missionary until you blazed a trail through jungle in central Africa, or survived the heat of a march through an Asian desert, or paddled upriver into the Amazon interior.

Of course, a part of your clothing outfit—the ownership of a pith helmet. It protected your head and allowed for some evaporation of perspiration in the head area.

Traveling on itineration in 2001, Mary and I stopped in Boulder City, Nevada for a service and visit with my sister and brother-in-law. He was privy to the sale and disposal of several boxes of pith helmets.

"Would you like to take one back with you to the Philippines?" he asked in jest, also in seriousness. "You could take four or five in your baggage for a couple of friends."

We noticed this downtown storage location was filled with innumerable boxes of this distinctive headgear. We thought of our beloved leaders and their need for such a usable and handy piece of equipment.

Shall we do it?" I questioned Mary, noting the twinkle in her eyes.

"Yes," she replied. "It should add humor to our business meetings. We could say this award is given in recognition of outstanding service rendered for the Philippines field."

We decided, since our annual meeting was scheduled for the end of December, we'll take some pieces of this unique equipment back with us. We considered, "If we take one helmet for each leader, their image will be greatly enhanced, especially as they travel about on ministry assignments. Even though we are in the modern age of digital gadgetry and cell phones, a pith helmet could be helpful."

The day arrived, Metro Manila, December 31, 2001.

I called the recipients forward; Mary read the citations.

[Russ Turney, Asia Pacific A/G Area Director] "Russ, you are in a position to set the fashion trend for your missionaries, while also needing to protect your shinny head from sunburn as you travel the world. It might be helpful to have this item near you when you drive on roads not on the map. We recall you once hurried home on backroads from Baguio to Metro Manila to rescue your family during an attempted coup.

58

We truly appreciate you and your life example of servant leadership. Thus, we present you your very own pith helmet."

[Bill Snider, Area Director, Philippines] Bill, you'll look great wearing this head gear in your videos and powerpoint presentations during fund raising in the U.S., and as you teach seminars in media on the field. We appreciate you as a person and all you do for us as our area director.

[John Balikowski, Field Chairman] John, this helmet will be an ideal piece of equipment as you leave soon for deputation. You can make it a part of your mission's display, to show at missions conventions, and even use it for an offering plate. And in between services, you can use this to transport your laundry to the laundromat! Thanks for your pioneering efforts and for a job well done.

[Mike Williams, Business Manager] Mike keep this in your office as a reminder of our gratitude for all you do for us missionaries. And as a reminder of the helmet of salvation you help the AGMF and ICI to present to a needy world.

[Wayne Benson, AGMF Annual Meeting Speaker, President of CBC, Springfield, MO] Wayne, we know you have a heart for missions and missionaries. You have traveled the world extensively, and now have the responsibility of influencing the lives of students for missions at CBC and elsewhere. So, add this item to your collection of mission's memories. Thank you for your Spirit-inspired, open, and sincere ministry to us.

[Mindy Demmer Carroll, Administrator, Baguio A/G Elementary School] Mindy, when we visited your school in Baguio, one of the classrooms had been turned into a jungle complete with trees and animals, both live and stuffed. As you supervise the school, you will now have your helmet for your "jungle." Thus, as the newest MK's come on the scene, you can pass on this great legacy to other boys and girls. Thank you for supervising and instructing our youth during these last few days at our 2001 annual meeting.

9. COUNTERPARTS OF TWO CHRISTMAS STORY CHARACTERS

(2014)

SEVERAL YEARS AGO I compiled a sermon describing the principal characters involved in the Christmas story and how each person or group reacted to the birth of Jesus. Some people expected great things from Him, some acted with indifference, other individuals hated Him.

However, an air of expectancy prevailed among those individuals who knew the biblical record. The Messiah appeared in bodily form as predicted.

One of the Christmas characters, Simeon, a devout and righteous man (Luke 2: 25-35), desired to behold the baby Jesus in his life-time. When he held the baby Jesus at the temple, he prophesied over our Savior to Mary and Joseph. Simeon stated in Luke 2:32 that Jesus was "a light for revelation to the Gentiles" and a light "for glory" to the people of Israel.

Simeon prophecies about: Jesus, the nation Israel, and Mary. First, Jesus will cause many persons to be saved. However, many people will not accept His testimony.

Second, Jesus will reveal the innermost thoughts of people in their own wicked life style. It will cause people to reassess and reevaluate their lives. Third, the body of Jesus will be pierced by a sword at His death—His death on the Cross of Calvary.

Simeon represents those people who read and believe the Scriptures. Consequently, these types of people expect great things from God and live lives of great faith. They believe exactly what God states in His Word. God proved Himself in their lives, and they expect Him to do exactly what He says He will do.

I think of Glen Berggren, age 76 plus (2014), a deacon in the Firth, Idaho, Tabernacle Assembly of God. To me, he resembles a 21st century counterpart to Simeon.

Mary and I had the pleasure of staying with Glenn and his wife, Elva, for one week after our itineration service in their church in September 2001.

Glen, a retired farmer, lives near Blackfoot, ID. He takes daily walks into the lava breaks that border the northeastern side of his ranch. Though retired, he maintains a well-ordered farm implement repair shop.

He also uses his repair shop to create masterful pieces of iron works, some of which have been placed on the first row of lava hills bordering his farm land.

Glen is not the ordinary farmer-type land owner. That is, one who may be found with several head of cattle grazing on adequate pasture land, tilling row crops, and maintaining sufficient maintenance sheds. I see him just as interested in life as a precocious second grader learning to use new computer software.

Glen, a delightful Christian brother, writes poetry, reads classic literature and poems, strums a guitar, sings, and knows how to use a computer. I see him as an early 20th century pioneer, who transitioned successfully into 21st century living conditions of the modern age.

He reads his Bible intently. Glen lost his first wife, Elva, a few years ago. She was ten years older than Glen. He remarried, continuing to live life to the fullest. I find Glen as a friend with whom I wish to communicate forever.

I see him as an associate who stands tall in wisdom, discernment, and political savvy. Glen loves life, is respected by his neighbors and friends. Like Simeon, Glen looks forward with expectancy to the second coming of Jesus.

Another character in the Christmas story, 84-year-old Anna, the prophetess, we see described in the Luke 2:36-38 account as a tremendous intercessor and prayer warrior. Known to be in the temple at all times, she worshipped, prayed, and fasted there regularly.

When she saw Joseph, Mary, and Jesus, like Simeon, she spoke to everyone around the temple area about the future redemption of Jerusalem by Jesus. A widow for probably 60 years, Anna represents the godly women in our own lives who receive insights from the Lord by the working of the Holy Spirit.

This kind of person has a hold on God that can help us in our personal lives, in our work, and in our ministries. God blesses these kinds of women who know how to touch God for various needs of our church families.

God blesses them by giving them a little look into the future, a word of wisdom about His plans for mankind.

Every congregation needs "Annas" praying and interceding for its members. These highly respected intercessors add stability and dignity to their congregations. They make decisions in fairness and equality affecting church members.

Nestled in the Bitterroot Mountain Range of the Rockies in the mining and forestry town of Salmon, Idaho, we met a similar intercessor during our itineration on February 11, 1981, 84-year-old Ethel Agee.

After dinner with the pastor and his wife in their home, we prepared to leave for our evening service. However, the pastor said, "Before we leave, I want you to meet a long-time member and intercessor of our church."

We followed him into a nearby room, where an elderly lady lay on a cot. All her worldly possessions seemed to be placed on a ledge by the window beside her bed. After the pastor introduced us, we learned she had been suffering for several years from an intestinal disorder.

She did not want the Lord to heal her, because "Then," she said, "I would need to find a job to support myself and get involved in worldly affairs. All of which would take away my time for daily Bible reading, prayer, and fasting."

She explained her involvement in intercessory prayer. In a previous year, their church had suffered from a pastor's neglect. She prayed him out of the position; he left in one month. Then, she prayed in another pastor in about a month.

Shortly, he, too, became negligent. So, she prayed him out of office, and prayed in another pastor in short order for their church.

We felt like we were standing on holy ground as she recounted these two incidents and the reason for her continuing illness. As we turned to leave, she turned to the window ledge, opened what appeared to be an old, but well-used cigar-sized storage box. She pulled out a one dollar bill, turned to us, and gave it to us for our ministry.

We felt a lump in our throats. Because of her sacrifice, it was difficult to hold back tears of thankfulness. She reminded us not to pray for her healing. Instead, pray for her that God would continue to use her in intercessory prayer for His glory.

We kept that one dollar bill for about six weeks before needing to spend it for an itineration expense. It seemed to us almost like a talisman, a good-luck piece, but more so like a bit of Holy Spirit anointed currency for use in only a real emergency.

During our next itineration in 1986, we visited Ethel in the Salmon Valley Care Center. Later, on our third itineration we learned Ethel had died in July of 1987 at the age of 90.

Who knows how many miracles, signs and wonders, she moved the Lord to perform during her lifetime. I only know, we felt a vacuum in our life after learning of her death. To God be the glory for her faithful ministry of intercession.

10. CHRISTMASES TO REMEMBER

(Reminiscences of a World War II Navy Veteran and His Wife, 2017)

SEVERAL COUPLES, AGES 85 TO 95, live in the Maranatha Village Retirement Center. For example, Bruce Gunn (known also as Sonny) boasts of his 96-plus years of age. His wife Elizabeth (known also as Pat) claims 93 years of age. March 22, 2017 marked their 76th wedding anniversary.

The Gunns, who lived in Detroit, celebrated a wonderful, but questioning and anxious Christmas in 1941, because of the bombing of Pearl Harbor. All the family gifts most likely weighted a ton. Bruce, Pat, and their three-month-old daughter passed on the beef jerky. Several siblings, cousins, the patriarchs, everyone wanted turkey.

However, dark war-clouds tinged the blustery December skyline. Bad radio news came from Europe! Would there be War in the States? Chances scant.

Bruce worked days as a machine repairman at Ford fulltime. Pat made ship parts during the war in the Detroit Diesel Plant. Yet, the eventually of war seemed faraway for each newlywed.

However, the lovebirds realized something terrible had occurred. Disaster at Pearl Harbor changed the lives everyone led. Bruce volunteered for life on the high seas. He preferred the Navy.

He attended boot camp at the Great Lakes Training Center, located north of Chicago. And graduated from the Navy Training School in Dearborn, MI as a Machinist Mate.

Gunn trained next in Rhode Island for PT (Patrol Torpedo) Boat action. Christmas 1943 left both Gunns fearful, yet with a hopeful state-of-mind, praying for a quick resolution.

Bruce served on PT boat No. 220, later on No. 297, in the Pacific Theater. These boats were 80 feet long, used aviation gas, could travel 60 mph and were designated as fast-attack craft.

Each crew member trained to use any weapon mounted or carried on deck. The weaponry included six 50-caliber machine guns, four torpedoes, one 40-millimeter canon, and one

37-millimeter canon. Bruce told everyone on board, he was the ninth gun on the ship.

The PT boats contained three Packard V-12 engines, each generating 1500 hp. The mission of the PT boats was to seek, find, and destroy enemy supply ships, freighters, and to shoot down planes, particularly the kamikaze aircraft, in harbors and on the open sea.

Bruce's letters to Pat arrived regularly and in the form of poems. Each creation glowed with sincere love and Gunn-type humor. His mind overflowed with stories that could fill tomes.

For example, for one anniversary he wrote as a crooner, With the title, "Many Happy Returns Honey." The poem stated:

"I would like to send you roses,

But just can't see my way clear.

So I will wish you lots of happiness,

On our anniversary, dear.

. . . . .

So it's just a card this time,

But maybe next time I'll be with you,

And present the roses in person,

The way I would like to do." (Excerpts from an undated 12-line poem)

Another poem stated: "To the Sweetest Girl in the World on Our Second Wedding Anniversary." [Bruce had not yet departed for duty in the Pacific.]

"I seldom think of spring and flowers

Nor bright summer skies so blue.

My thoughts always wander to just one thing.

My thoughts always wander to you.

. . . . .

Winning you for my bride,

For to me you mean just everything.

My joy, my life, my pride.

But I guess these words can never express

Just what I would like to say

Nor the feeling I have for our baby and you.

And the prayer I whisper each day,

That this war will soon be over.

[Signed] From a Grateful Husband"(Excerpts from a 43-line undated poem)

Bruce spent Christmas 1944 in the area of Leyte and Mindoro, Philippines. PT boat duty had kept him in the Mindoro area for a second Christmas.

On one foray, Sonny piloted their PT boat No. 220. He inadvertently crossed a coral relief – a "no, no" activity. Group Commander Kallonell awarded him the Monal Shaff laced with a coral cluster (8 January 1945). The card of acknowledgement stated: "for distinctive stupidity."

Thus, he became recognized as an official member of the "Reefer's Club." The purpose of this tongue-in-cheek award-ceremony emphasized the necessity for the use of safety procedures at all times.

His storytelling capabilities and humor inspired several cartoons penned by Peter Wells, a syndicated war cartoonist, who served on PT boat No. 297 with Bruce. Two such large cartoons depicted Sonny as he "reefed" their boat.

One of Sonny's undated poems describes the abysmal loneliness and disheartening bleakness of a sailor's life. Although undated and untitled, I will call it: "The Blackness

of the Incoming Cold Fog."

Bruce wrote to Pat:

"Have you ever stood a watch

Aboard a blacked-out ship,

And stared into the blackness

Wishing for a safe trip?

Charles T. Clauser

You keep lookout all around

While standing up on deck,

And wondering how you'll make it,

Wondering what will come next.

You watch the waves roll by,

See a white-cap now and then,

And feel the air get thicker

As the fog comes rolling in.

You listen to the wind,

It sounds weird rushing by,

You turn your eyes to heaven,

There's no moon up in the sky.

Then you look out at the sea,

While the rain beats in your face,

And the night air grows colder,

Almost freezing you in place.

You start to cuss the Navy,

But it's time for your relief.

So you let your buddy suffer

While you go get some sleep."

At last, VJ Day, September 2, 1945." We're going home!"

Christmas 1945 ushered in a jubilant family reunion. First, the Gunns ate a leisure breakfast in their Detroit home. Next, lunch activities were undertaken at Pat's parent's home and included partial gift exchanges.

The evening meal time activity continued at Bruce's parent's home. It included more gift exchanges and fellowship by all the family members present.

Bruce, however, gave his life to Jesus on March 2, 1943 while still on PT boat patrol during a harrowing attack and skirmish with two kamikaze airplanes.

His post-WWII activities included attending a Central Bible College [CBC Springfield], extension Bible School program at Brightmoor Tabernacle in Novi, MI, a suburb on the north side of Detroit.

He was ordained in 1965 by the Assemblies of God, and received his 50-year service pin and certificate on May 20, 2015.

Sometime later, during his ministry at Brightmoor Tabernacle, he penned an undated, salvation poem entitled:
"You've Chosen Your Own Place." Stanzas six, seven and three
of seven quatrains read:

> "At that Great White [Throne] Judgment seat
>
> You will your maker face:
>
> 'Depart from Me! I know you not!'
>
> You've chosen your own place.
>
> Oh come, my friend, just as you are,
>
> The Savior's Grace receive:
>
> The Law made null, a home on high.
>
> If only you [would] believe.
>
> 'Tis offered freely by our God
>
> That you His son may be.
>
> If you refuse the Son of Light,
>
> His grace no more you'll see."

Following those horrific war years, with the Lord's
help, Bruce made something good out of his life. He blessed
countless thousands of persons, through a fruitful church ministry at Brightmoor Tabernacle, later renamed Brightmore
Christian Church.

He served first as a youth leader, next as an assistant pastor, lastly as a pastor to seniors. Jesus empowered all his ministry responsibilities there over a 55-year period. To God be the Glory

11. OUR PAL MIMI

(August 10, 2015)

I

A S I GROW OLD, I still recall your face.
You loved to play outside in our backyard.

I threw the Frisbie far for you to chase.

We also walked around the park, small pard.

For there on swings and slides and jungle bars,

We watched those breathless acts of doggie skills,

'Twas even on command away from cars.

You liked to run and jump for daily thrills.

A lost rear leg, the car you did not see.

We prayed and knew you'd run again, dear pal.

But sorry, no more jungle bars with me.

I'll throw your ball, for catch and fetch, sweet gal.

Our little Mimi came to us a mix.

All white, a cuddly, bright-eyed pup with lots of licks.

II

We opened Christmas gifts galore one morn.

One wrapped gift sat between your paws—a toy.

Your tail, it wagged and thumped, no looks forlorn.

A bell-in-the-ball, you played with utmost joy.

When traveling to Mary's parent's home,

Or out the other way to visit mine,

My friend you always whined and barked and roamed.

Both you and our child performed near the same loud kind.

When placed in the back of our car, it allowed us to load.

No fret, no problem as we packed the Ford.

There, mutt on blanket, child in pen, we rode.

The miles, passed safe and long each way—thanks, Lord!

Your days of youth, we all felt jubilant.

You made our family so relevant.

III

We turned off main street, Grandpa's home appeared.

On cue you woke, sat up, your head held high.

Our child clapped hands and sought the man revered.

Now off the long road, what joy to find this guy.

Whenever Grandpa's car went out for mail,

He took our Mimi, his "helpful" riding pet.

To guys, a cup of tea to tell a tale.

Companion pal, his bud, felt no regret.

For Asian work we heard the Lord assert,

Assignment Philippines (1982) to teach God's Words,

We left dear Mimi, old and weak—she hurt.

With Mary's parents thinking, "You're both nerds!"

Old "Arthur-ites" made each day a fight.

You tossed and turned, a terrible sad sight!

No choice, but to the vet's seemed only right,

And Grandpa grieved so much, he teared, "Good night!"

12. FAITHFUL FRIEND AND TIRED
TEACHER'S DESK

Fiction:
(In Clauser A/G Missionary Newsletter, December 15, 1988)

THE SCHOOL BELL CHIMED the start of activities on this last day before Christmas vacation, the 21st of December. "Two minutes, children," Miss Haynes reminded them. Anticipation beamed in their eyes.

Unnoticed, Faithful Friend walked with care, between the playful children returning to their seats. Each student asked the other near him as the bell signaled a start of the activities of the last day, "Did Miss Haynes invite a guest to our party? Do we know this man?"

The presence of their unannounced visitor interrupted the conversation of the Teacher's Tools standing together on top of the worn face of Tired Teacher's Desk.

The sound of their clomping boots and rain-drenched coats placed on racks near the front of the room, signaled to Tired Teacher's Desk, the start of this last festive day before Christmas recess. Their morning ritual of trooping in through the squeaky, classroom door began promptly at 8:00 a.m.

"Oh-oh, gro-o-an," Tired Teacher's Desk sobbed. "For 43 years, the owners of those dirty, scuffed shoes have been kicking the varnish off my bruised body! And those dripping rain coats sloshed gallons of water all over my table-top face. My stain marks look terrible! It's like standing in a shower after you combed your hair and powdered your face.

"Someone . . . anyone . . . please, help me! Hmmph! No one has any concern for me. They just don't care! Doesn't anyone love me? Oh, where did my Faithful Friend go? I know He cares!"

"Perhaps, my Dear, I should write a stern letter to Brother Long-Face Principal," Miss Soft-Lead Pencil exclaimed. "He always listens to me. Yes, that's it. It won't take him long to tidy up this intolerable mess of muddy boots and soggy raincoats."

"Listen here," Mr. Red Ink-Pen interrupted. "A job like this needs a professional writer. My qualifications are more acceptable than anyone else for priority jobs like this situation. I can highlight this communication and call Brother Long-Face Principal to action imm-mediately! I know he will not let the face of Tired Teacher's Desk be vandalized anymore by those little urchins!"

"Highlight, did I hear you say *highlight* your request?" Grandpa Green-Marker squeaked. "Stand aside young fellow. This action calls for a seasoned veteran, who experienced years of calling people's attention to the important issues in student essays. I will take the appropriate action in directing Brother Long-Face Principal's attention to this custodial matter."

"I think your thesis sounds presumptuous," Sister Straight-Ruler sneered. "In fact, none of you ever received the complete support of Brother Long-Face Principal. Why, I was the last one placed in his calloused hands! He uses me to establish standards of conduct for the occupants of those big boots and water-soaked coats. They measure up to my guidelines when I'm around. Brother Long-Face Principal sees to that!

"Ladies and Gentlemen, my friends and co-workers," Mrs. Antique Letter-Opener rasped. "Let me assure you, Brother Long-Face Principal will not read nor act upon your well-intended actions unless I take time to open the letters for him. And today, I'm very busy. We do not waste time and effort to open every letter that comes to his desk.

"You must remember, Brother Long-Face Principal, a most busy man, can't be bothered with every whimper. I think

Tired Teacher's Desk is out of order. She cries for your sympathy. Have you forgotten how we remedied the situation three years ago? Faithful Friend helped solve our problems."

"Oh-oh, gro-o-an," Tired Teacher's Desk bawled again. "Those dirty boots will be my ruination yet. Boo-hoo! No one loves me."

"Patience, patience, my dear companion," compassionate, Miss Soft-Lead Pencil pleaded. "We'll soon find a way to preserve your stained, table-top face. Just wait until our Faithful Friend comes again. I know He will have an answer for us."

"Who do you think would take time to cooperate with you two?" brash Mr. Red-Ink Pen retorted.

"Hey, th-a-a-at, just might be the solution," wise Grandpa Green-Marker surmised. "We each have our assigned jobs. If we pool our talents and resources, I think we can convince Brother Long-Face Principal to keep the Boot Brigade and that drippy Coat Company off Tired Teacher's Desk."

"It hurts my pride," chattering old-Dog Stapler yelped. "But, I suppose . . . well, I might try this teamwork . . . once, just once, mind you. Cooperation, you know, has not been one of my strengths, because I prefer to work alone."

"Perhaps, I've been too legalistic," Sister Straight-Ruler mused. "Old, worn-out Tired Teacher's Desk has suffered beyond recognition this last year. She does need our sincere prayers and help. Those energetic youngsters seem so thoughtless."

The Teacher's Tools had forgotten about the increasing presence of squeaky shoes, drippy boots, and innumerable soggy raincoats piled beside Tired Teacher's Desk. They became absorbed in their own conversations, unaware of classroom events.

But now, school began, the class was called to order. Everyone expected a joyous day of singing and pageantry. Everyone knew a party would soon begin the Christmas celebration.

Then, silence . . . .

As He approached the front of the classroom, Faithful Friend turned slowly around beside Tired Teacher's Desk, and with gentleness, patted her drenched table-top face. He looked with approval at the Teacher's Tools standing at attention near Him. Miss Haynes spoke to Faithful Friend as she stood beside Him.

"Welcome to our Christmas party. Class, please stand and greet our guest."

With a dignified air of love in His countenance, it seemed He spoke to each individual: "I experienced loneliness these last three years and could not come to join you. Thank you for the invitation to bring me back. I've felt so lonely these last three years, not being able to join you."

He observed their new concern for one another and remarked, "My name is Jesus. Your love and cooperation with each other made possible my return to this glorious birthday celebration."

13. A CHRISTMAS TANNENBAUM

(A children's story for persons young in heart who desire to know more of Yuletide traditions and the object of our adoration in the Advent season. September 15, 2011.)

GRANDPA, WAKE UP!" Little Bits creaked in the crisp December morning air.

"Small one, the sun must warm my arms before I may move," the old tree responded.

"Grandpa, where did those men take my brother, Shorty?"

"A family of five humans came and picked out Shorty as their Christmas tree this year. I heard them say they lived nearby, over by Cloverdale."

"Will they bring Shorty back to us after Christmas? Will he grow again among us?"

"No, little one. Instead, they plan to decorate each one of his beautiful arms to celebrate the birth of the Christ child, Jesus."

"Sounds foolish to me. Our friends, Whistling Cardinal and Loud-Mouth Blue Jay, even Camille the Chipmunk, I think, added magnificent color to Shorty's gracefulness. But what— who started this custom of burdening the arms of fir trees?"

"For two millennia, our ancestors gave themselves in sacrifice for this custom to observe the birth of Jesus, our Creator and Lord."

"Do we have a choice? I mean, will every one of our brothers and sisters end their lives in removal from this hillside for the joy of those two-legged ornery kids and axe-happy hulks?"

"No, my dear. Some octogenarians, like me, remain alive to assist in the development of new generations of Christmas trees, or to produce healthy logs for homes of these humans, or to stand as resident protectors for the wildlife who dwell among us."

"Do you mean those men will come and separate us – even abuse us, maybe destroy us, or cause the breakup of our family? Why? What did we do wrong?"

"Nothing, youngster. We grew up in this special forest farm for a purpose. Our mission in life, our existence on this hillside, our duty for Mister Caring Hands, supervisor of life on this entire mountain range, demands we grow tall, straight, and attractive."

"I don't think I understand. As a teenager, I don't see things yet from your perspective. A little squirt like me needs new experiences each day in order to survive. Mission, purpose, duty—Grandpa, what do you mean?"

"We live in an extended family, Little Bits, of celebratory Christmas trees, of logs for houses, and of forest shade trees."

"Grandpa, will someone or some family of humans come and choose me for their Christmas tree? Or, will I stand alone, grow tall, old, and perhaps lopsided like you, with a home for squirrels and skunks under my feet?"

"That decision remains a possibility. Many of our kinfolk served with distinction in one of those capacities. Others found themselves measured in the sawmill down by Charley's Hollow and sent on the railroad to Pebbles Center. Those of us who remain on this slope, lift our hands each day to praise our Jehovah-Jireh."

"Grandpa, all I want to do each day: just bask in the sunshine and provide shelter for those rambunctious baby birds and chipmunks that fly and flit around us. I find solace in their presence."

"You show maturity already, child. We, in this grove learn to serve others, sometimes through pain, oft times with joy. Like Jesus, who followed the way of the Cross,

His service culminated in a personal sacrifice. Each day we follow His example. It means giving our lives in service to others."

"Mom tried to explain these goings-on to me as a responsibility, an obligation each of us live with, before they took her down to Charly's Hollow."

"Your Mom stood tall as she observed the pain experienced by our other family members. She, however, like other Moms, became a comforter and helper for the younger ones among us. I miss her, too.

You see, young lady, as Tannenbaums, as majestic fir trees, we provide usefulness in myriad ways to a world that needs our help.

"In one way, our sacrifice points to the life of Jesus as we become Christmas trees for His glory. He allowed Himself to undergo crucifixion in order to provide forgiveness of sins and salvation for those humans who accept His provision of eternal life. Humans use us as reminders of that sacred act."

"Grandpa—those men, here again. Ouch! That hurts! Grandpa, please help me. Where will they take me? Will they return me to our hillside? . . . Oh, Grandpa, please tell Sissy, bye for me."

"Remember my darling, wherever they take you, God loves you."

It seemed but a few moments later when Little Bits began her contemplation. "Sissy, do you remember? Twenty-seven years ago the Nickelhausers planted me by Shorty in their front yard.

"He lived to see sixty-one Christmases before that terrible rash blighted his arms and blotted out his life. Inexcusable. Mr. Nickelhauser didn't consult with Supervisor Caring Hands in the early stages of the disease.

"I still grieve over his demise. Imagine, Shorty cremated piece by piece, limb by log in their backyard fireplace, an unforgettable sight.

"Well, since Jesus has a place in heaven for these redeemed humans, and I assume their animals, I believe he will set aside a glorious hillside for us.

"Sissy, how wonderful. We grew up from the same pine cone, thanks to Uncle Jack Squirrel. His voracious appetite passed over our buried location near Sammy Stone.

"And, I remember the day Mr. Caring Hands replanted several of us saplings close to Grandpa. Both knew well our need for water, food and companionship.

"I appreciate the opportunity to stand in the Nickelhauser front yard, and on a clear day, see Grandpa far away on our hillside home, able to wave his withered arms in greeting.

"The dear old fellow, 107 years old; look, he still knows us. No senility veils his ability to communicate.

"My sister," Little Bits continued to speak out loud to herself. "How nice we grew up together, side by side, able to give the Nickelhausers memorable pleasure at Christmas time as they decorate our clan.

"Each year they add new adornments to honor the Christ child. Even their neighbors admire our distinctive December coats, prepared for us to accentuate our praise for the Lord Jesus.

"But it unsettled me for days, my arms drooped, several of my needles fell off when I saw you, removed by lumberjack surgery and carted off to Charley's Hollow.

"Later, Sissy, I regained my composure when I saw you, aah, near naked, then placed on the front porch and steps of the Nickelhauser home. You were used to replace broken sections of the floor, and thus became a life saver for them. They held you in high regard.

"Sissy, as I reminisce about our family obligations, I feel I shall live for today, its opportunities, its challenges. I find it difficult to realize the events of which I speak, transpired twenty-three years ago.

"Since then, Grandpa fell over and broke apart in the terrible wind and ice storm of January, ten years ago. And you, dear buddy, my closest friend, burned to ashes last night in the

Nickelhauser home, which men with the two Cloverdale fire engines could not extinguish.

"Tomorrow? Tomorrow will dawn for us to celebrate another Christmas. Jubilant young Tannenbaums rejoice these days in our front yard with their new responsibility.

"However, I soon may join you, Shorty, and Grandpa on that hillside in heaven, because my bark—now separated and thin, my sinews—separated and unstable, my needles—bleached and brown.

"Nevertheless, until that final call comes Sissy, I shall continue to worship Jesus as long as I can raise my dilapidated arms in adoration even while the winter wind whistles through me.".

14. A SKINNY SKUNK CELEBRATES CHRISTMAS

(A children's story; December 12, 2015)

MOST PEOPLE KNOW the tongue-twister story of the skunk and a stump. If not, the jingle begins: "A skunk sat upon a stump. The skunk thunk the stump stunk, and the stump thunk the skunk stunk."

For greatest effect, however, these lines must be spoken quickly. For example [read or speak rapidly]: "A skunk sat upon a stump. The skunk thunk the stump stunk, and the stump thunk the skunk stunk."

To better understand this tongue-twister encounter, I present, herein, the following event as a 1910 Christmas conversation between a sour-smelling, skinny skunk, Sylvester, and a sorrowful, shabby, pine-tree stump, I call Sylvia.

In that decade, a small, year-around stream crisscrossed the mile-wide valley through Farmer Flemming's cattle ranch where he grew alfalfa, corn, oats and wheat.

In the middle of his spread, a narrow, one-way bridge allowed passage for area neighbors to cross-over the meandering creek and take a short-cut to Pipestone, the nearest settlement, just two miles over the ridge behind Farmer Flemming's ranch house.

Each year Farmer Flemming left a small portion of his fields near the bridge, unharvested for the purpose of growing weeds, brush, and groves of various shade trees, which became home for pheasants, quail, partridge, occasional deer, and small animals. Therein, lived silver-tipped Sylvester the skinny skunk.

Years earlier, fat Farmer Flemming cut down four towering pine trees near this site, including Silvia's stately erect body, and shaped them for beams in order to build his bridge over Mann's Creek. This wandering waterway widened near the Flemming barnyard and allowed wading. But on the downside of the bridge, several large pools of water supported crappies, bass, and rainbow trout.

One December day, stinky Sylvester, the skinny skunk slunk sidewise toward Sylvia. The sad and stained stump, now robbed of vitality, appeared rotted with age, and rendered ruthlessly full of holes by boring beetles and cut-worms.

"Sylvia," Sylvester squealed, "one more day and we can celebrate the birth of King Jesus."

"I think in one more day," Sylvia responded droopy-eyed, "I shall see Jesus face to face. There's little life left in my scarred body. My roots no longer take in nourishment," she stammered quietly.

"Cannot happened," Sylvester shouted with eyes wide open. "You know Frau Flemming brings her table scraps to their garbage pit near the bridge. Her left-overs have provided fine meals for me and several of our forest friends. Why, Sylvia, your roots take nourishment there, too. Right?"

"Yes, little friend, but now my roots are drying up. I'm dying."

"Oh, Sylvia, you're my best friend in this grassy glen. How can it be?"

"Hush now, youngster. The forest changes daily. It's a new day."

"But what will I ever do, if I can no longer sit on your shoulders? You've been my best buddy, my most faithful friend and helper ever since I could walk."

"Sylvester, we both must look to Jesus for His loving care every day. Me, because I will not live in this world much longer. You, because you're very young and need guidance in the days ahead."

"Well, I do want to learn more about the good life in the Lord Jesus."

"You will, indeed, little one. Plan to learn more about life from Farmer and Frau Flemming and his family, especially when they come for their once-a-month, Sunday summer picnics or their winter ice-skating parties."

"Yes, I know it will be a gala Christmas celebration this year when the Flemmings bring their eight children and are joined by their neighborhood families."

"Sylvester, they sing the Word of God in beautiful harmony. Many of their songs come right out of our Bible."

"I enjoy their singing of those happy songs. While I sit in the nearby bushes, I listen to those wonderful hymns."

"I believe you've learned something already about Jesus."

"Yes, for sure. I know He is one important man in everyone's life."

"You observe life well, Sylvester. But know this, He created you and me and all our forest friends."

"Oh Sylvia, those words make my head spin. I need to sit on your shoulders again in order to consider what you said."

For now, Sylvester, just remember we will see each other again in His heavenly home. . . Oh, I see Jesus coming for me!"

"Wha. . . Sylvia, what's happening?"

"Goodbye, Sylvester. Jesus just called me home!"

"Sylvia? Oh my! Gone!

"Well, I must listen to the Flemming family to learn more about Jesus.

"Perhaps they will tell me about Sylvia's disappearance. My friends in the forest will quiz me and want to know. I must be able to tell them the truth about Sylvia's going away. Jesus, please help me understand

II. SOUL-SHAPING SENTIMENTS

1. A ROAD TO NOWHERE

(Written 2010)

CLAUSER," I THOUGHT to myself, "watch your step! Keep yourself spread out and low on this loose shale. If it moves, you will immediately plunge 30 feet over this cliff with a gigantic pancake splat into Manila Bay.

If you claw for safety at those pieces of rock to your left, that cliff may tumble down and bury you."

I had just made the difficult decision to proceed along this pathway, which quickly became *A Road to Nowhere..* I had expected to walk leisurely to a nearby beach and search for sea shells.

I felt confused as my mind tried to process conflicting thoughts: "Did not the Corregidor Island map show a road traversing this section of the four-mile-long, tadpole-shaped, World

War II fortress, which in earlier years had guarded the entrance to Manila Bay?"

This route I soon learned had changed drastically after 50 years of abandonment. "Why were these ten-inch-in-diameter trees growing in the middle of the road?" My map, I decided, was exceedingly out-of-date.

"Careful now," I continued fearfully, "move only one limb at a time! Distribute your weight evenly. Look ahead, not down the cliff. Choose the spot where you will place a hand or foot.

Stay focused on crawling slowly forward, no sudden movement. Do not stand up. Step deliberately. Lord," my mind pleaded, "I need your help."

Mary and I finished dinner at the hotel during the previous hour, which concluded our two-day missionary meeting and touring of Corregidor, including an exciting visit to the three levels of the war-scarred island:

Topside with its parade ground, museum, and bombed-out one-mile long barracks; Middleside with the remains of the enlisted men's barracks and the hidden water storage placed under the tennis courts; Bottomside with its piers and hotel; the Malinta Tunnel with its light-and-sound show depicting the WW II history of the island.

I knew the boat would leave for the 21-mile return ride to the Metro Manila harbor in two-and-one-half hours. Checking the island map and remembering our tour ride yesterday, I had located a beach that looked promising for collecting sea-shells.

Years earlier, a fellow missionary had enticed me to begin collecting sea shells. It was an enjoyable pastime. Where ever we traveled in ministry throughout the Philippines, I picked up or acquired a few new shells.

Of the approximately 50,000 varieties. I felt privileged to have acquired a couple hundred various kinds of these beautiful objects. The textures and sizes intrigued me because of the wide range of design on each shell.

When I decided to begin this excursion, I told myself: "by taking this short-cut, I can accomplish my 'shelling' adventure and return to the hotel in sufficient time to meet my wife and board the boat."

But, danger!

"We're almost there, Jesus! Two more steps," I thought to console myself, "and we'll be off this chalky outpouring of shattered rock. Don't rush it Charlie Boy! Take your time. Easy, move deliberately, Charles."

My mind raced frantically: "Here I am, 60 years old, and I'm acting like an undisciplined eight-year-old youngster. Yes, Jesus, I should have turned back before attempting to cross that outcrop of shale."

This large mound of shale probably broke off because of explosions inside the mountain near the Navy Tunnel complex in the south side of the entire labyrinth of tunnels. Several side tunnels intersected the main tunnel, but after WW II only a few had been cleared of mines and debris.

These tunnels were originally designed for storage of war materials, but in WW II the underground system housed a battery of city services utilized at different times by both combative sides.

As a bastion of strength begun in 1922 and completed in 1932, Corregidor's WW II history became legendary and remained in utter ruins before tourist renovation began in 1985 by the Philippines government.

"Forgive me, Lord," I prayed continuing my walk. "My desire for more sea shells has over-shadowed my common sense. Well, I'm not going back over that pile of shale. If I did, I might end up sliding off the cliff and swimming with sharks.

Or those jagged rocks might leave my mangled body as fish food. I see no rescue boats in sight, not even a nearby porpoise willing to save me if I slip over the drop-off.

The hot mid-afternoon tropical sun continued to bake me. Wiping my forehead, because of the summer heat and my self-inflicted stress, my persistence continued overcoming good judgment: "I'm going ahead," I rationalized. "Surely, this road will connect soon with the entrance to the Malinta Tunnel."

"Whoa . . . What happened to the road?" My mind was exploding with disbelief. "I see only trees growing where this portion of the mountain slid down to the sea shore.

How will I maneuver down through this maze? Why, this situation looks worse than crossing the shale.

Let me see . . . Yes, I'll slide slowly down to that tree. . . . Now, I can maneuver over to that big tree. Careful . . . left foot, cross over the right.

Oh, Lord, please station your angels around me. I don't want to arrive back at the hotel with my backside and pockets full of mud."

I had lost track of time, but finally negotiated down the steep muddy hillside thickly covered with willow saplings. I felt like I walked, climbed, and maneuvered through a box of gigantic upended toothpicks, which provided hand holds allowing me to lower myself to the rocky beach, but which had no semblance of a path.

Lord, I gasped in my thoughts. "This beach won't allow me to go 'shelling.' I see no wading area, only more jagged rocks." However, I did now see the desired beach some distance ahead.

But to my chagrin, there was a large 40-foot high rock abutment jutting into the sea between where I was standing and where I desired to go 'shelling.'

"Oh boy," I found myself contemplating. "Wading around it will not be an option, neither swimming past it. Oh, my watch tells me I had better be heading back to the hotel. Departure time for Manila begins in little more than one hour."

"Lord, I need you again! I have only one option, climb this hillside through all this waist-high brush." Confusion reigned in my mind. "Lord, you've never left me nor forsaken me. Jesus, help me again, please, as I climb through these low bushes.

"Don't let there be any cobras or poisonous rice snakes down by my feet. I can't even see my shoes because the stubble has become so thick.

I'm climbing by faith, Lord. And please, don't let spiders, big or small bite me as I climb up through these stalks.

"Give me strength, Jesus, my legs are turning to rubber. I'm not used to climbing a 300-foot high mountainside covered with every imaginable obstacle. And please don't let me step into a hole, break a leg, or fall into an old WW II submerged or partially open pill box. I don't need a cement fox-hole tomb."

Huffing and puffing all the way up the mountainside, I finally reached the top of the side hill. Only in the last few yards did the brush thin out that I might look down and see my feet.

With relief, I stepped out on the paved road about 100 feet from the front of the Malinta Tunnel entrance. I purchased a soft drink at the nearby snack bar to quench my thirst and rested a moment to regain my composure.

With a sense of urgency, I respectfully asked the guard to take me through the 925-feet long and 25-feet wide main tunnel, since I needed to meet my wife at the hotel and catch the late afternoon return boat ride.

He understandably and courteously agreed without hesitation. Usually, visitors pay to walk through the Tunnel and view the 30-minute, light-and-sound show. We instead, walked quickly toward the light at the far end of the Tunnel.

As the guard used his flashlight to guide our way, I lifted my thoughts heavenward: "Thanks again, Lord, for rescuing me several times during the last two hours of my stupidity. And Lord, please help me act responsibly from now on."

When I arrived back at the hotel, with dirty hands, smudged face, multiple scratches, cuts, and muddy pants, my wife looked at me aghast and in shock. She loudly exclaimed: "Where in the world have you been?"

2. EVANGELISTIC FERVOR BY THE SEASHORE

(1983)

Virgie commented, "I prefer to cook in our kitchen with charcoal briquettes. Estella likes to use wood for her cooking. We alternate days in preparing meals." Virgie Cabasag, head pastor, and her associate Estella Garcia, alternately shared the responsibilities of Christian preaching and teaching in their church in their small Muslim village.

The Minanga Assembly of God, a seaside congregation, located six kilometers southeast of General Santos City, first met as a Bible study in 1971.

These two young ladies led this emerging church work full time in South Cotabato immediately after their graduation in 1979 from the Assembly of God Bible Institute of Mindanao in GSC.

Estella grew up in Minanga and accepted Jesus during her first year at Bible school. Her father, Jose Garcia, was the first person in the village to accept Jesus as his Lord and Savior due to the 1970 ministry outreach of AGBIM students.

My purpose for travelling to GSC (1983) included the teaching of two on-site, master's-level extension courses at AG-BIM for the Far East Advanced School of Theology based in Metro Manila.

The two courses were taught back to back, each for a two-week period of time, five days each week, three hours per day. Virgie and Estella attended those two classes, and later, completed their master's degrees at the Asia Pacific Theological Seminary (formerly FEAST) which relocated to Baguio City, Luzon, a mile-high mountain site among the pine trees of northern Luzon.

This group of sixteen pastors and district leaders came from several different places throughout Mindanao. A close bond formed between most of us, both men and women, over the twenty-five years that my wife Mary and I ministered in the Philippines.

When petite Virgie and stalwart Estella first invited me to minister in their church in 1983, nine families attended, representing 20 adults, 16 young persons, and 35 children.

"The population in our fishing village," Virgie said, "consists of 73 families." These ambitious ladies set a membership goal for the next year at 150 members. "If accomplished," Virgie noted, "our goal would give us more than one-third of the persons in the community."

Estella clarified their desire to increase attendance, "by six families in 1984, and by 15 additional families in 1985. In

1989, 18 families attended with 70 water baptized members. Eighty-nine persons attended regularly."

Estella remarked, "No other religious organization conducted church activity in our *barangay* (village) in 1983." The community of Minanga numbered 107 people in May 1983; 400 persons lived in the village in 1989.

In 1989, however, three other groups had begun recruitment activities. In 1983, there were only two Muslim homes; in 1989, five Muslim families existed in the village.

Virgie commented, "When we started our work, the Muslims controlled our village, but not now. And when we have special events at our church, like dramatic presentations, some of the Muslims will attend.

"Drama," Virgie explained, was the best method of evangelism in 1983, a life story of someone, not a Bible character. It was followed by an altar call.

In 1989, Bible stories, Vacation Bible School, and drama were used for evangelism. We have used VBS materials for ten years. Now in its second year, we also conduct a two-week church camp each April or May. Several parents attend, because their children participate."

A special relationship developed for Mary and me with Virgie, a lady with an infectiously pleasant smile, and inquisitive-minded Estella. We returned regularly to GSC in the following years to teach other short-term classes as adjunct faculty members at AGBIM (later renamed, the Mindanao Regional Bible College).

During those various teaching times, MRBC President Segundino Ladura, acting as our interpreter, drove us in the college Jeepney to area A/G churches for Sunday morning evangelistic services.

With each trip to GSC, we scheduled a service or teaching seminar with Virgie and Estella at the Minanga A/G, a fifteen-minute, covered-tricycle ride from the downtown market in GSC.

Both co-pastors attributed their church growth to prayer. As a result, the Mananga residents gave both ladies noticeable moral support.

The Women's Ministries in their congregation involved themselves in evangelism activities and neighborhood improvement projects, while four men of the church, when not out fishing, constructed a new church building.

Sister Virgie compared their congregational emphasis on stewardship and prayer in 1979 to its effectiveness in 1983. She acknowledged, "Members and attendees who practice stewardship and invest time in prayer, realize that God blesses them by increasing their catch of fish and by healing sickness in their homes.

In 1983, church members only gave one-half of their tithe. In 1989, they had learned to give a 100 percent tithe."

On my first visit, the two co-pastors gave me a tour of their home. They lived in a three-room home, made of bamboo, wood, and woven coconut leaves. It included a bedroom, a living room, and a kitchen.

The "comfort room" (toilet) and an enclosed bath area were attached along the outside of the house. The walls of the house were made of matted bamboo leaves, the floor of split bamboo poles. Quarter-inch slits in the bamboo floor provided needed air ventilation for the hot tropical weather.

The two pastors kept their books and clothes in glassed-in wooden cabinets as a protection from the wind, rain, humidity, and insects. Their parsonage lawn, a soft blanket of beach sand, became the domain of two dogs, one cat, a flock of tame geese and a small goat,

The come-and-go activities of inquisitive children found the place a wonderful playground, because of the congestion of nearby homes standing nearly side-by-side to each other.

These *pastoras* (female pastors), therefore, practiced Jesus' commandment about children stated in Matthew 19:14. "Let the little children come to Me, and do not forbid them; for of such is the kingdom of heaven."

Estella added, "Our men in the church bring water to us from the one community source, a 150-foot, deep-well located at the west end of the village."

Next, I noticed a kerosene lamp in their living room. Estella explained its use. "One liter of LPG gas (1.057 quarts) will burn for ten hours, which gives us light for two evenings, 6-11 p.m."

Fishermen in the village depart in their boats around 4:00 a.m. each morning, seven days a week, from the seashore area in front of their homes. They return around noon. However, when they find a certain school of fish running, they may return to sea later in afternoon and come home at 8:00 p.m.

Many fishermen, if successful, may go out for periods of up to six days. The type of fish sought most in the waters of the Sarangani Bay is the Yellow Fish, a junior-sized tuna.

After my first visit to Minanga, I wondered, "How many of us would be as dedicated to our ministries as these commercial fishermen remain to their vocation? Would we go fishing for souls all year long for Jesus, regardless of the type of catch available?

Could we rejoice in times of leanness when the catch might draw barely a net full all week long? Would we remain faithful and focused, when the schools might run heavy?

Two talented and energetic ladies went down to the seashore southeast of General Santos City to cast their nets for souls. The Holy Spirit still brings in the catch.

Today, innumerable men and women in Minanga Buayan know their eternity as a definite reality in Jesus, thanks to the evangelistic efforts of Virgie and Estella.

3. THE TURQUOISE SASH:
TRADITION AND MARIOLATRY

(1989)

EVERY WEEKDAY MORNING she walked down the hill on Derby Street in the White Plains subdivision of Quezon City, Metro Manila at precisely 5:35 a.m.

Always immaculately dressed in a white blouse and skirt, this middle-aged matron descended in a regal manner, head held high, with an umbrella hooked on her right arm and a worn black-covered Bible cradled close to her body.

Our eyes met but for a short moment. I greeted her with a polite smile and a cordial "good morning" each time we passed by each other. I was jogging up the hill as she resolutely descended the paved incline, while the dark turquoise-colored sash at her waist swished from side to side.

At each daily encounter, she managed to smile a greeting. Although one time she momentarily stopped me and asked: "What time is it?"

This pleasant morning, I could contain my curiosity no longer. I had pondered why she always wore white and had that same particular green sash wrapped around her waist. It was draped in an impeccable manner down her left front side.

"Excuse me, please," I spoke patiently, as our eyes met again near the hilltop. "May I ask you a question?" Without waiting for a reply, I pointed at her flowing sash and inquired: "Why do you always wear white? And, what does that sash signify?"

I was embarrassed. It had taken a lot of courage to be that bold with someone I'd never officially met. It was not the thing to do in Filipino culture. But this morning, I just felt like engaging this nice appearing lady in a short conversation.

She responded quickly in excellent English, with eyes twinkling, "Why, that is the design and color of the sash that the Blessed Mother Mary wore when she appeared to people at the Lourdes Grotto!"

Her reply caught me off guard. Without hesitation, she began a Mariolatry discourse. There was hardly a moment for her to take a breath in her rapid-fire lecture. It was impossible for me to make any comments about Jesus.

"Oh yes, I believe in Jesus," she added as an afterthought. Her way of stating the fact reminded me of an animist approach to religion. A conglomerate attitude—don't leave anything out that might bring good luck and favor. We exchanged a few religious pleasantries before going our own ways.

Throughout the unusual discussion, I discovered she had been walking down the hill every morning for a 6:00 a.m. mass at Christ the King Catholic Church located outside our subdivision near the back gate of White Plains. The next morning, Friday 5:35 a.m., she informed me, "it was not a Bible cradled in her arm, but a Missal."

She emphasized again the importance of Mary's humanity: "God could not have become a man without the very important humanness of the mother Mary."

My reply stated Jesus became the central figure in the Bible and Mary only a minor character. There are over 300 prophecies about Jesus. Every book of the Bible points to Him. I reminded her of John 14:6: "Jesus is the way, the truth and the life" (NKJV).

On the second morning we conversed, she had asked my name. Then kept talking about Mary and the last words Jesus spoke from the Cross: "Dear woman, here is your son," and to the disciple "Here is your mother" (John 19:26, 27, NIV). At last, she volunteered her name: "Myrna, they call me 'Merka' for short."

Our short encounter was interrupted by a beautiful green car with darkened windows that stopped beside us. She quickly stepped into the front seat.

I barely had time to say: "Have a good day" before she left. I understood her desire to leave. We both were late that morning in our regular schedules. Attending mass consumed her mindset in order to please Mary.

I pondered these two chance meetings as I continued my jogging. Next time, I thought, I must follow up with the question: "What is truth?" I prayed the Lord would allow us to meet again. I wanted to show her Mark 3:31 and Matthew 12:46-50. In that passage, Jesus said that his disciples and those persons seated around Him were His mother and brothers: "Whoever does God's will is my brother and sister and mother" (Mark 3:34, NIV).

Three days later I learned her nickname was "Amerika." Her given name, Amerna de Guzman. Now 60 years old, she lives with a cousin. She had been a dentist for many years, although not currently practicing. Born in Metro Manila, the family on her mother's side was involved in medicine.

She had never married. Today was the second time I had reversed my jogging route and walked down the hill with her. She appeared patiently cordial, so I continued to question her.

In the previous week she had given me a little brochure entitled: "Catholic Replies to Protestant Errors." I planned to give her a written reply the next day, the Lord willing. However, it never happened.

It was almost two weeks later on the *barangay* (subdivision) election day, I asked Amerika if she ever attended an

Easter sunrise service. She replied: "No, we celebrate the *Salubong*." (*Salubong* celebrates the meeting between the Blessed Virgin Mary and the Risen Christ on Easter Sunday.)

I kindly informed her as we walked along that morning, four women were mentioned by name at the tomb on Resurrection Day. No Gospel account mentions Jesus' mother by name. She perhaps was a part of the "others" (Luke 24:10).

Mary Magadalene receives mention in all four accounts; Mary the mother of James receives mention twice and was referred to another time; Joanna and Salome each receive mention only once. If Mary, the mother of James were Jesus' mother, it would have been stated.

Amerika's feeling approved the Catholic mix of tradition with the Bible. I asked, "Why as a dentist, would you fill a cavity on the right side of a person's jaw when the pain was on the left side? Or why would you perform a root canal when all that was needed was the repair of a small cavity?" She felt there was no harm at all in mixing tradition with biblical knowledge and fact.

I commented: "Traditions change, people change, even the traditions of the Central Philippines are different from the traditions of the Northern Philippines." I tried to be courteous in my observations. "I know you desire more of God in your life."

"No," she stated. "I don't want to be like God. I had thought she wanted more of His holiness in her life, but apparently not. She desires to emulate Jesus' mother, Mary. As we continued talking, I walked outside the back gate this time, even to the far corner of our housing area.

In the days following, as I walked down the hill and continued my early morning conversation with "Merka," I realized she speaks all the language of a Christian, but can't pinpoint a date on which she repented of her sin and gave her heart to Jesus. I came to understand, she still believes her salvation was accomplished by works.

On another day, I met "Merka" halfway up the hill again during my morning run. I stopped momentarily after our greeting and said to her "Remember, salvation happens by faith, not works." I repeated the phrase twice. She had become a very communicative person and allowed me to walk and speak with her.

A few days later she stopped me and asked my name and exactly where I lived. I walked down the hill and out the back gate with her again. We reviewed "old positions." I saw no change in her religious views over the eight months (February to September, 1988) in which we interacted with each other.

I pray the Holy Spirit will change her mind, not to rely on works, Mariolatry, tradition and custom for her salvation, but to realize by faith only Jesus Himself will satisfy her quest.

4. THE ROLE OF MUSIC IN THE CHURCH

(1984)

MY ESSAY, *The Role of Music in the Church* appeared in the Philippines' Bethel Bible College Yearbook, *Kala-wili* (meaning: accord, unity, harmony), March 1984, page 55. I wrote: Christian music has its basis in Scripture.

Paul summarized in 1 Corinthians 14:15: "I will sing with the spirit, and I will also sing with the understanding" (NKJV). He meant our Pentecostal music expression should be Holy Spirit inspired.

Holy Spirit inspired church music tells a story. Human interest abounds in the song *Christ Arose*. Good church music presents a testimony and helps bring people to acknowledge Jesus Christ and their need for salvation. Songs like *Standing on the Promises* and *Amazing Grace* have touched the hearts of thousands of individuals.

Successfully used church music includes prayers set to music for either congregational or solo use, such as *Come Holy Spirit*. Songs like *Great is Thy Faithfulness* teach doctrine and carry a definite message to be learned.

Some songs assist us in worshipping and praising God. *How Great Thou Art* has become one such highly-favored praise hymn.

Meaningful church music expresses love. *Love Lifted Me* and *Shepherd of Love* help us raise our thoughts heaven-ward. There are songs that warn us of judgment to come, that anticipate Christ's return, that assure us that God sees, knows, and cares about each one of us. Other songs greatly bless us and tend to give us a surge of strength.

Music prepares the mood of the service and for giving comfort in times of great emotional stress. Church music has the role of assisting the altar call at the time of invitation.

Whether music exhorts us to Christian action, helps us express gratitude to God or strengthens us in Christ, a vibrant, heartwarming music program projects a message of life.

Church music should do four things. It should inspire us to lead a dedicated life of unselfish service. Next, it should en-courage each one of us through times of discouragement and despondency.

Music used appropriately teaches various foundational truths. Lastly, music in the church should always point to and glorify our Savior, Jesus Christ!

Psalm 150:3-4 admonishes us: "Praise Him with the sound of the trumpet; praise Him with the lute and harp! Praise Him with the timbrel and dance; praise Him with string instruments and flutes!" (NKJV).

We are to praise and worship God with all of our music resources. David said in Psalm 13:6: "I will sing to the LORD, Because He has dealt bountifully with me" (NKJV).

The Pentecostal church has long recognized the vital and essential element of its music ministry. It must continue to be a vigorous and captivating part of evangelistic, preaching-teaching, and revival outreach.

A deeper understanding of the ministry of church music will include the use of hymns, gospel songs, and scriptural songs.

(These comments were not placed in the above article because of space limitations.) A hymn presents a song of praise or adoration to God. Hymns are people's songs.

They are sung by the congregation and teach doctrine. Hymns are the center of church music, because of being directed to God. By contrast, a gospel song tells a story about someone or gives some kind of message.

Gospel songs are songs of the heart, very melodious, singable, and well-suited for evangelism. Gospel songs are directed toward unbelievers through (1) witness; (2) testimony; and (3) a challenge. These songs place emphasis on an appeal or invitation to some kind of action.

Many times gospel songs are composed by a novice for both its words and music. A gospel song states a simple, direct truth, which has frequent repetition in one stanza.

These songs are readily understood by children and are easy to remember, created to reach the emotions, and to provoke a decision in the heart.

A gospel song may be a folk song, free in form, emotional in character, devout in attitude, and evangelistic in purpose.

Ephesians 5:19 speaks of singing psalms, hymns and spiritual songs. A psalm (or scriptural song) represents an inspired text given to man by God. A hymn presents a person's expression of praise, thanksgiving, and prayer unto God.

A spiritual song, (a gospel song, or a chorus) becomes the vehicle used for testimony to tell others of God's goodness and blessing in a person's own life.

We need all three types of songs—psalms, hymns, and spiritual songs, sung in each of our services.

5. OUR CHRISTIAN LIFE-STYLE

(A speech delivered at First and Calvary Presbyterian Church, Ecumenical Men's Prayer Breakfast, Springfield, MO, May 16, 2012)
Introduction.

THE LORD JESUS SAVED me February 15, 1973 at my age 39. The next year I went to Bible school after previously having earned a Ph.D. in music education. I began my career directing high school bands, then college bands, followed by a time of work in college administration.

Charles T. Clauser

In August 1982, my wife Mary, and I began a 25½ year missionary ministry as teachers in the Philippines.

Like many other Assembly of God missionaries, we performed a variety of ministries in those years and afterward retired to Maranatha Village in 2006. Now I spend time involved in my writing projects and playing trombone in the Maranatha Village Chapel, Sunday evening orchestra.

I title these devotional thoughts today, "Our Christian Life-Style," and invite you to turn to my text, Romans 12:1-2. I shall read from the NKJV.

"I beseech you therefore, brethren, [The NAS says, "I urge you."] by the mercies of God, that you present your bodies a living sacrifice, holy, acceptable to God, which is your reasonable service.

[Verse two] And do not be conformed to this world, but be transformed by the renewing of your mind, that you may prove what is that good and acceptable and perfect will of God."

The Message paraphrase states these two verses: "So here's what I want you to do, God helping you: Take your everyday, ordinary life—your sleeping, eating, going-to-work, and walking around life—and place it before God as an offering. Embracing what God does for you is the best thing you can do for him.

"Don't become so well-adjusted to your culture that you fit into it without even thinking. Instead, fix your attention on God. You'll be changed from the inside out. Readily recognize what he wants from you, and quickly respond to it. Unlike the culture around you, always dragging you down to its level of immaturity, God brings the best out of you, develops well-informed maturity in you."

I have chosen this self-examination passage in Romans, because it encourages each of us to give our own life a regular analysis—like going to the doctor for an annual check-up or taking the car to the garage for its periodic oil change and inspection.

These verses in Romans promote guidelines for holding on to a firm relationship with our Lord Jesus Christ. Therefore, I want to relate a few situations from our ministry in the Philippines to illustrate this well-known passage of scripture.

First, Present Your Bodies a Living Sacrifice, Holy, Acceptable to God.

I remember one service I conducted in Glan, a small town not too far from the southernmost tip of Mindanao. I spoke through an interpreter on Matthew 24, concerning end-time events. At the end of my presentation, I gave an altar call for salvation and later for healing.

To my amazement, two mothers came forward for healing prayer, each with one breast bared, each one nursing an infant child. Now, I grew up in central Idaho, a farm boy on a small acreage. This scene shocked me. I almost lost my concentration and focus.

I had not expected a demonstration of motherhood in this manner. I learned later this type of activity was standard operating procedure for that part of the Philippines. Thinking about the incident afterward, I realized those mothers knew best how to keep their babies quiet.

I suppose carrying around a small drapery cloth would just add baggage to their mobility. Also, we had conducted the service near the equator where nights remain hot.

I somehow maintained my composure and kept ministering along the prayer line that evening. I resolved to stay absorbed in my purpose for being there—caring for the needs of both the mountain people and the flat-landers in the congregation.

I felt praying for the needs of these kind people and speaking to them about the mercies of God, an honor and a privilege.

First, Present your bodies a living sacrifice, holy, acceptable to God.

Second, Do Not Be Conformed to This World.

I spent almost 17 years ministering part and full-time to the students and faculty at the Bible Institute for the Deaf in Metro Manila. At one of their chapel services, one of our international evangelists ministered the Word of God, followed by an altar call for students to rededicate their lives to Christ.

As the prayer time continued, two male students began to slither and writhe on the floor like snakes. And, another student began to turn cartwheels across the floor at the front of the assembly.

The evangelist and I prayed, bound, and cast out the demons causing those satanic activities. Then, those deaf students rededicated their lives to the Lord. The ministry that morning turned out to be hard work. But guided by the Holy Spirit, and in Jesus' name, we did not let those three precious young people remain conformed to the world.

Allow me to jump ahead a few years to 1995, and relate how a WW II guerilla became conformed to Jesus. I met 69-year-old Filipino pastor, Charlie Umengan, while on a ministry trip organized for a small group of pastors and members of his host congregation in the mountains of northern Luzon, just a short distance from the internationally well-known rice terraces.

Charlie, at age 17 in 1943, had become a Philippines guerilla and served three years on active duty with the elite Sierra Madre Mountain Wanderers Guerilla Army. The war, however, had interrupted his studies in the second year of a college medical program.

Toward the end of the war, his American commanding officer was killed as his Filipino company made an assault up a hill in an attempt to retake the Dalton Pass. The 89 members of his detachment had no rank, but after the American's death, they made Charlie their commanding officer.

Those guerillas, I think, had no rank, because at their homes, they could fade into the everyday life of farming, etc., then regroup at night for their resistance activities. When I met Charlie, he was the only member of his company still living. Amazingly, by that time, he had pastored for 45 years.

After the war, our missionaries along with those of other denominations, flocked to the Philippines. One of our well-known lady pastors conducted services in Charlie's home area, April 1, 1949.

He swore allegiance to Jesus that Good Friday in the Ilagan Assembly of God, Isabella province, while still wearing his wartime Colt 45 revolver strapped on his hip. Charlie said: "I saw lightning and fire following Mayme Williams' face and hand movements as she preached."

He became her first convert in that church. Then he went to Bible school, against the wishes of his father who disowned him. However, a few years later his father had a change of heart, recanted and reconciled the broken relationship.

Charlie's beliefs and existence demonstrate the spirit of a person who decides to change his life-style from the ways of the world to the way of the Cross.

First, Present your bodies a living sacrifice, holy, acceptable to God.

Second, Do not be conformed to this world.

Third, Be Transformed By the Renewing of Your Mind.

On one ministry trip, I flew with my interpreter from Metro Manila to Puerta Princessa City, on the island of Palawan. We continued our journey southward by bus, speaking in some of the rural A/G churches along the way.

In one of those services, a lady came forward for the healing of a large, grapefruit-size goiter protruding from the left side of her neck.

During the altar call time, several of us prayed—time after time for her healing, probably over a period of forty minutes. Nothing happened! I prayed; each of the four or five pastors present prayed. No response! We each took turns, but finally quit praying, exhausted from the ordeal.

A few weeks later as I reflected on the situation, it dawned on me, "I should have inquired of the lady if she knew Jesus as her Lord and Savior." Because, I began to consider the possibility, *I believe she was an unsaved mountain tribal lady.*

Thus, I realized I had placed the cart before the horse. In this situation, I should have asked her first about her relationship with Jesus before beginning that healing prayer.

It may not be necessary to check that factor in other needs for healing. But in this case, I became convinced in my spirit, she needed Jesus before we started to pray for her healing. I believe it would have made a difference that night in the outcome of our prayers for her.

I also questioned myself, "Had I prepared well spiritually for that ministry trip?" Possibly. Maybe not. My pride may have stood in the way. However, in all cases, Jesus is the Healer. I felt it a hard-learned lesson.

During the last ten years of our time in the Philippines, I had the opportunity to distribute a large number of Bibles and tracts to assist in training many of our pastors. I gave literature also to members of congregations, participants in district meetings, as well as tracts to street children in Metro Manila.

This activity ensured that pastors in certain areas of the Philippines, where we had scheduled regular visitation routes, now owned a complete Bible, which included both Old and New Testaments.

These pastors were admonished to see that all their Sunday school teachers, board members, and other church leaders received copies of these basic Bible study tools. The reason for our distribution program: most people in those areas had very little cash flow. They could not afford to buy a Bible.

On one of those trips, we traveled north of Subic Bay, the former U.S. naval base on the island of Luzon. When our visitation ended that day, I still had one Full Life Study Bible left in the car, not yet dispersed.

My pastor friend and interpreter, Leroy, said, "We have a church near here, about four blocks off the highway. I would like you to give him this Bible." After the formalities of greetings and introductions, I presented the middle-aged pastor with this last Bible in our possession.

As soon as he clutched the Bible in his hands, he jumped up and down, and exclaimed, "I have been praying for a copy of this particular Bible for two years." That experience made my day.

On the three-hour trip back home, I rejoiced and praised the Lord, knowing many lives would be transformed and renewed because of that pastor's diligent study and preaching of the Word of God.

First, Present your bodies a living sacrifice, holy, acceptable to God.

Second, Do not be conformed to this world.

Third, Be transformed by the renewing of your mind.

Fourth, Prove That Good and Acceptable and Perfect Will of God.

One block-session class Mary and I enjoyed co-teaching in our district Bible schools was the Christian Family. When completed at various locations, we conducted a wrap-up session during the last class meeting for gathering comments and evaluations.

It became a party. We made arrangements for refreshments of cookies and ice cream, which served to end the class in a good mood.

We often ask the question during those social gatherings, "Now that you have completed the Marriage and Family class, do you feel like getting married someday?" I remember one young man responded, "Definitely no!"

Another young fellow exclaimed with enthusiasm, "Yes, sir. I want to have 12 children—three sopranos, three altos, three tenors, and three basses. Because, when I go out to pastor a church, I want to have my own family choir." If I remember correctly, one of the girls made an aside remark to a friend, "Issh, I hope he will seek the will of God!"

Prayer becomes an important aspect of any missionary work and I will illustrate this point with another well-remembered highlight from our ministry. One weekend during our first four-year term in the Philippines, we were invited to minister in the Word and in music, at a house church located in a suburb on the northern side of Metro Manila.

Three single ladies co-pastored this body of believers. They had placed about 50 folding chairs in the front yard of their home. An awning tied to trees covered a portion of the seating area and provided a modicum of shade. I stood near the front door to present the message and Mary sang with a cassette tape accompaniment.

After the service the three ladies invited us into their home for dinner, a usual custom for this type of situation. We enjoyed the meal, which I like to say, included petrified chicken—that is, very well done fried chicken with no possibility of salmonella or worms.

A person almost needed a saw to cut through the outer portion of meat. Our conversation flowed freely as we became better acquainted. We learned in our conversation, the three ladies wanted to marry but had no immediate prospects.

I said, "Well, we can pray right now for the Lord to take care of that situation. God will hear our prayer." We prayed; the young ladies giggled, partly in disbelief, yet hopeful.

I can report that within one year, each one of those three pastors had found the right man and married her prince charming. Yes, God answers sincere, honest, meaningful, and acceptable prayer.

The mercies of God amaze me, even today. Jesus only asks for our cooperation. Therefore, may each of us enter into a regular life-style check-up, such as we read in Romans 12:1-2, to ensure God's anointing in the continuation of our own ministries.

I conclude by reaffirming: To God be all glory, honor and majesty. I praise His mighty Name.

6. SIXTY YEARS IN MINISTRY
WITH NO REGRETS

(Compiled July 16, 2012)

PASTORAL-MINDED OCTOGENARIANS and nonagenarians at the Assembly of God Maranatha Village Retirement Center have not lost their caring vision for souls. They still live with the desire to energize young people for ministry and to continue in service, albeit limited, for the Lord Jesus Christ.

Their thoughts, after receiving a 50-year service pin and recognition for 60 years of ministry, resonate with reflections of past victories. In similar ways, each pastor interviewed said, "I have no regrets. If I could, I would do it all over again."

For example, ninety-one-year-old Stewart H. Robinson, born January 17, 1921, in Hot Springs, SD, a WW II US Air

Force veteran, graduated from Central Bible Institute (CBC), Springfield, MO in 1951.

He received recognition in 2012 from the Southern Missouri District A/G for 60 years of service. "Robbie" pastored for 50 years, including 30 of those years as an international missionary evangelist who ministered in 59 different countries. His wife of 63 years, Rose Louise accompanied him on every one of his overseas trips. (Stewart died April 11, 2013 at age 92.)

He spoke as the evangelist for the Blackwood Brothers during a one-week assignment in Africa as a result of their periodic singing in Calvary Temple, Springfield, MO, where Stuart pastored for 13 years.

Stewart remarked of his 50-year recognition, "I had some real setbacks earlier in life, but the Holy Spirit impressed me to keep on, keeping on."

Looking back on 60 years of ministry, he stated, "I have no regrets. I served my country, teaching navigation for B-24 bomber personnel during WW II, and I served my God, and my family."

Stewart's advice for Bible school students, "Don't try to take the front seat. Serve others. The preacher's appearance must invoke the attention and respect of the body of Christ. Be a sponge. Learn everything you can."

Eighty-year-old Melford J. DeVries, born June 21, 1932, in Willmar, MN, graduated from North Central Bible Institute (now NCU) in 1953 and received his license to preach in 1952 from the Minnesota District.

He joined the North Dakota District A/G in 1955, which awarded him a 50-year service pin in April 2002. He and his wife Harriet were married for 56 years, from June 12, 1952 to 2008. (Mel died November 24, 2016 at age 95.)

Mel confessed in disbelief about the receipt of his 50-year pin, "I couldn't believe I had survived that long. I wear the pin, however, with pride as a member of the Assemblies of God.

One of my most enjoyable ministries was serving as the North Dakota District Secretary/Treasurer for three years (1962-1965). I learned that ministers need more fulfillment than just performing their pastoral duties."

This year (2012) marked his 61st year in ministry. He commented, "I began working with the A/G Stewardship activities in 1977 and soon became the national director of the Financial Trust and Stewardship Department, later renamed Deferred Giving and Trust. I enjoyed this ministry because it provided service to families for the finalizing and the resolution of their estates."

Mel expressed these thoughts for ministerial students. "The Lord is coming soon, and we should be about His business. The principal focus of our efforts is to point people to the plan of God—salvation for their souls.

"I want them to realize the future is greater than the past. To be ever present with the Lord in heaven is our principal objective. This is what I have been saying all my life. The message has never changed."

Ninety-one-year-old Jewell E. Tucker, born November 9, 1921, in Springfield, MO, worked on the Frisco Railroad Line for five years as a journeyman mechanic and, afterward, attended Central Bible Institute (CBC).

He received ordination on November 20, 1951, in the Kansas District. He transferred into the Illinois District in 1961, from which he received his 50-year service pin in 2001. The Tuckers came to Maranatha Village in 1998. He enjoyed marriage with Ruby Josephine ("Jody") for 63 years (1941-2004). Jewell died November 9, 2012 at age 96.)

Of 60 years in service to the Lord, he said, "It has been a great life. I would do it again." His explanation about constructing and pastoring the Lyons A/G in Kansas (1953-1956), fired up specific recollections, "The people were wonderful. We kept in touch with some of them for a long time."

One highlight of Jewell's ministry—he raised money for Teen Challenge, Chicago, for eleven years. But from 1974-1987, he raised money for the Revival Time radio program and the Turning Point TV programs.

Jewel said of the Turning Point programs, "I picked out suits for the men; my wife Jody picked out fabrics for the ladies clothes."

Jewell spoke of this lesson for pastors and Christian workers in training, "It is important to be sure of your calling. When the hard times come—and they will come—whether or not you are in ministry, be sure to live the Christian life because the enemy, Satan, will try to destroy you. Remember though, God will seek, save, and help you."

Eighty-four-year-old B. Thomas Bozarth, born November 11, 1927, in Springfield, IL, a WW II US Navy veteran, graduated from Southern California Bible College, in Pasadena (now Vanguard University) in 1950.

He received his 50-year service pin in May 2004 from the Illinois District. Of this award he stated, "I had just come out of the hospital from open heart surgery for a five-valve bypass. I immediately got a bacterial infection from the surgery. As a result, my weight went down to 117 pounds."

Tom and his wife Glenna clocked 67 years of marriage as of August 5, 2016. After 64 years of ministry since his licensure in 1948 by the Southern California District, he explained, "The date came sooner than I expected. However, I would do it all again. (Tom is 89 as of April 2017.)

I particularly enjoyed my evangelism activities of starting a new church, my juvenile ministry with the Los Angeles City Sheriff's Department, and later working with a Teen Challenge youth program.

"As missionaries, we ministered in the Marshall Islands and in the Solomon Islands with its 67 different language groups. In the latter island chain, we formed a 'Hallelujah Hill' congregation, in a thatched-roof church, planted in the middle of the battlefields on Guadalcanal, which kept two separate denominational congregations together as one unit worshiping and praising the Lord."

Tom continued with this admonition, "If I were speaking to students in a chapel service, I would counsel them—check, and make sure your call comes from God. Seek God's will and do it in his power and presence. Do it in obedience, trust, and faithfulness to God. Be open and sensitive to God's direction.

"We can only expect His blessing as we are obedient to His call. Be dependent on Him. Don't give heed to anything 'anti' to the cause of God's voice in your life. God's call for me is far different than yours. My call was to fill a gap out in the Asia Pacific island region."

Eighty-four-year-old Robert E. Allen, born January 20, 1928, in Newcastle, IN, fulfilled his WW II duty as a member of the US Maritime Service. Both Bob and his wife Norma Lee completed Berean Bible School correspondence courses in order to be ordained by the Church of God, Anderson, IN, in 1953.

Beginning in 1952, they spent thirteen years in church building and church planting in Hawaii. (Bob is 89 as of April 2017.)

During that time, Bob studied and became a journeyman electrical engineer and passed the test as a master plumber. Bob and Norma Lee celebrated 68 years of marriage (2016) from the date of joining their lives together on May 10, 1948, in Tucson, AZ.

Both Allens received their 50-year A/G service pins in 2006 as members of the Arizona District. This year (2016) will mark 65 years of ministry for them. They spent 35 years as missionaries with all their assignments in Pohnpei, Somoa, and in Hawaii.

Norma exclaimed, "I was shocked at the time, but honored to receive a 50-year service pin. I didn't feel worthy, but was grateful because I realized the Lord had blessed us. We were proud to be a part of a people who really believe in the Lord and who believe in being filled with the Holy Spirit."

Bob emphasized, "The Lord performed many miracles in our ministries, especially in Pohnpei. For example, our first Thanksgiving dinner in Pohnpei consisted of a can of Franko-American spaghetti. We had been there only one week.

"The next day we were asked to pray for a lady in the local hospital. Her leg was scheduled for amputation, but because of gangrene, the Lord healed her completely. As a result, she invited us to her home for a Bible study which instantly became our first church on the island."

Norma Lee commented, "If I was speaking to Bible college students, I would emphasize the need for a close relationship with the Lord and obedience to His call in each person's life. We must give our total life over to God. He will be faithful.

"I see a bright future for young people today. I believe God will anoint them and give them a greater anointing than we had in our ministry. I know God will do something great for them."

Bob added, "If I was conducting a Bible study with young people in a coffee house, I would tell them, 'Answering your call is worth it all, no matter what you face. You can't depend on programs. You simply have to dig down deeper in your spiritual expression, because of things you wouldn't know how to deal with.'

"Stay with the doctrines we believe in—salvation, healing, etc. It's God's will to heal us—not if, but He will heal us. He will heal all our diseases today as He did back in the time when he walked on earth."

Eighty-three-year-old Daniel T. Raught, born May 8, 1929, in Seelyville, PA, attended Metropolitan Bible Institute in Suffern, NY in 1947 and received his license to preach in 1950 from the New York District, originally named the NY/NJ District.

He received his 50-year service pin in 2003 from the same district. He and his wife Marjorie will celebrate 62 years of marriage as of September 9, 2012.

Dan explained, "I enjoyed our ministry because it centered in our involvement with people. I think the people enjoyed us, too, because we invested ourselves for 25 years in one church and 12 ½ years in another church.

In those years, we tried to comfort and encourage the people in these congregations. We have good memories of all the churches in which we served."

Dan spoke of their ministry as a team effort. "My wife served faithfully in women's ministries and played either the piano or the organ in our services. When we worked with the youth, we both used puppets; I did ventriloquism.

I led in worship and regularly played trumpet. Sometimes Marjorie and I would sing duets. Afterward, I would preach."

Dan offered these thoughts for students attending Bible school today. "What do you visualize yourself doing in the years ahead? If you don't have a definite calling, do your best to please the Lord. Tell Him, 'Lord, I'm here to do your will.'

"The Lord has imparted something into your heart to do for Him. God's plan for each of us will be good. Some people have a dream or a vision, but not everyone will have that experience.

"Don't be rebellious to anything God may offer up for you, but try to please Him. Follow His leading and He will seek to fulfill your life in all avenues of your endeavors. If you desire to be used in the ministry, remember your wife will have an important ministry with you. So, choose your mate well."

Eighty-four-year-old Wesley E. Reynolds, born October 19, 1927, in McCook, NE, a WW II US Navy veteran, graduated from Central Bible Institute (CBC) in 1953 and received his 50-year service pin in 2005 from the Southern Missouri District.

He and his wife Miriam celebrated 68 years of marriage on November 25, 2016. (Wes is 89 years old as of April 2017.)

Licensed in 1953, and ordained in 1955 by the Nebraska District, Wes will observe 64 years of pastoral ministry in 2017.

He recounted the beginning of his ministry, "I was so thankful I found the Lord early in my life, because I grew up as one of twelve siblings in a rough family situation.

"However, an evangelist came to McCook, NE, where I grew up. Almost all our family members received salvation through the time of his meetings in my hometown.

"Looking back, I praise the Lord for His amazing guidance for giving me many productive years of ministry that included preaching, teaching, and counseling. For example, we bought property and built a church in every assignment. I can say we tried our best to closely follow the leading of the Holy Spirit in each ministry situation."

Looking ahead to students now in school, "I would tell ministerial students today to find an older minister or person who will act as their mentor, a guide to help in spiritual battles and who can reveal pitfalls to avoid in personal relationships.

"Take your ministry one step at a time each day and be a good listener. First and foremost, be a people person.

"In practical matters, do preach on finances and tithing, these areas concern a person's life. Highlight missions. Exhibit stick-to-it-ive-ness in street meetings and in participation at community activities." (Wes died May 9, 2017 at age 89 years.)

Eighty-nine-year-old William F. Farrand II, born January 19, 1923, in Flint, MI, a WW II US Navy veteran, graduated with a diploma from Eastern Bible Institute in Green Lane, PA (1949), a bachelor's degree from CBI (1970), a master's degree from the Assembly of God Graduate School (AGTS, 1977), and a doctor of theology degree (Th.D) from Trinity Theological Seminary, Newburg, IN (1986).

Bill was licensed in 1949 and ordained in 1952 by the Michigan District. (Bill is 94 years old as of April 2017.)

He received his 50-year service pin in 2002 and recognized for 60 years of service in 2012. The Michigan District presented him a plaque for 45 years of service as a MI District missionary. Bill and his wife Alvera celebrated 67 years of marriage as of November 23rd 2016. Alvera died July 22, 2017.

"God has always orchestrated our lives," Bill said. "For example, as a 4-year-old, curly-headed kid in Flint, MI, I remember attending a service in my home church, Flint Riverside Assembly, when a man lying on a cot with a broken back was taken to the platform.

The pastor and congregation prayed for him. He immediately jumped up and ran around the auditorium, which resulted in a Jericho March.

Bill reflected on his Asia Pacific assignments, "The Lord sent us to Kandy, Ceylon (Sri Lanka, 5 years), Cebu and Metro Manila, Philippines (24 years), Fiji (3 years), and back to Columbo, Sri Lanka (2 years). During our first time in Ceylon, I tutored Coltan Wickamaratne for three years.

Coltan later became their district superintendent and then an international evangelist. We were called out of our first retirement and sent to the Fiji assignment. After our final retirement, I served ten years as chairman of the Retired A/G Missionary bi-monthly meetings in Springfield, MO."

Bill explained, "I was a senior pastor of seven churches for short periods of time in Michigan and in our Asia Pacific assignments, including the military church at Clark Air Base in the Philippines. These ministries embraced a variety a nationalities, including Chinese.

"I would tell ministerial students today to love the people and teach the Word, because it has power to change people and solve problems when anointed by the Holy Spirit.

"I've written at least a dozen books, mostly about theology and Christian living. I order a few copies at a time from Lulu publishers and give them to whomever expresses interest."

Whenever these retirees tell their life story to Bible school students and speak of their challenges, tears, heartaches, stressful moments, answered prayer, and victories for Jesus— pastoral ministry classes benefit and will be set on fire for the Lord by the power of the Holy Spirit.

What a wonderful, productive heritage these seasoned veterans can pass on to younger generations by their wisdom, examples of courage, and determination to see souls saved for the cause of Christ!

7. HERE'S WHAT THEY DO AT AGE 90!

(Compiled originally on February 1, 2013.)

THE LIVES OF EIGHT nonagenarians residing in Maranatha Village minister to others beyond hindrances of bunions, bulges, bridges, blemishes, and baldness. Do these stalwart souls expect to live as long as the Hunzas of northern India, who reportedly live to the age of 130 or more years? Only the Lord knows. I asked each one, "What inspires you to keep-on, keeping-on for the Lord Jesus Christ?"

My neighbor, Michigander Bill Farrand, age 94, and married 67 years to Alvera, wrote about 20 books concerning theology and prophecy for former students. Macular degeneration now diminishes his ability to read or write. Bill said, "My computer replaced my pulpit; these days I can only preach to my computer."

During his 45-year missionary career, he fulfilled the duties of a college president in three Bible schools in the Asia Pacific region.

Bill's prescription for longevity: "Continue to maintain a good attitude and engage in meaningful family interaction, covered with much prayer."

My Nebraska neighbor, Bob Bolles, age 95, telephones and gives greetings to residents in MV on their birthdays and anniversaries. Each phone call is highlighted with prayer, congratulatory comments, and a personal word of encouragement. Thus, Bob's primary love language employs the affirmation of words.

Bob and his wife Virginia celebrate 71 years of marriage. He grew up on a farm near McCook, NE, served as a naval officer and pilot for 23 years, flying twin- and four-engine aircraft. For another 23 years, he served as a real estate appraiser.

For longevity of life, he recommends, "Live a positive and consistent life style that considers the feelings and needs of others before committing to your own desires, especially in marriage. As you establish a healthy routine of eating, sleeping, and daily activities, develop a pattern of ministry. Be a servant for Christ."

A Minnesota friend, Estella, age 98, shared married life with E. M. Clark for 71 years. In her growing up years, she was the youngest of seven children. Her hobby of playing piano by ear in those early years, later graced many of their church services and sectional meetings. A hobby she pursued in MV was the giving of perms, trims, or the styling of hair on a limited basis to a lady friend. (Estella B. Clark was born November 4, 1918, died February 27, 2017 at age 98.)

The Lord used Estella in active support ministry for her husband, especially during his ten years of service as the Illinois Assemblies of God district superintendent and his ten years of service as president of North Central Bible College. Her purposeful acts of service engendered this comment, "I worked hard in life; E. M's. job became my job, too."

She would encourage others, "If a person seeks a fulfilled life, exert self-discipline and maintain spiritual discipline." Her counsel to achieve these goals, "In whatever decade of life you may be living, you must know you are where God wants you. So, be friendly, always happy, and be a good helpmate."

A North Dakota friend at MV, Avis Osland, age 95, shared marriage with her husband Chester, for 57 years. One of nine children, she became blind in her left eye at the age of two. After graduation from North Central Bible College, she began preaching and received her license to preach in 1941. (As of April 2017, Avis was 99 years old.)

Her husband, a preacher and a cabinet-maker and carpenter, often preached in one location; on the same day she would travel to another church and preach.

Throughout her life, she wrote many articles published in magazines and newspapers. Her ministry today, because of hearing loss and diminished eye sight, entails "a life-style of prayer for her friends, family, and missionaries."

Avis described her legacy as, "the showing of interest in other persons and the offering up of prayer, which can facilitate their receiving of the Lord's grace and love in time of need or a period of discouragement."

Farmers work hard in Iowa. The process of raising a bountiful crop begins early in the morning and can continue until late at night. Ninety-one-year-old Leo Fish and his wife Margaret, from Le Mars, married for 71 years, can attest to years of keeping their shoulder in the harness, praying for the Lord's blessings, and giving out more in service to their community than the rewards received.

Managing their 240-acre farm required constant attention. In order to meet the farm expenses and assist his four children in attending college, Leo also sold either Caterpillar tractors or Harvester silos. Later, he bought the patent to manufacture the Eberhardt Silopress. This latter activity took him to several countries overseas as well as throughout the United States.

Leo didn't stop farming until age 80. Twelve years ago, he suffered a stroke which brought on some memory loss. Upon his recovery five years ago, the Fishes moved to MV. In this last decade, he served as an usher at Grace A/G in Springfield.

His comments to all persons below the age of 90, "Whatever you do, do it with all your heart. Look at the end goal. Reach out to help people and be an example of Christian service. Husband and wife must live and practice the same mindset. Follow through with a disciplined Christian work-ethic in all the activities of your life." (Leo Fish, born August 9, 1922; died January 11, 2017 at age 94.)

Ninety-six-year-old Stanley M. Horton, married to his wife Evelyn for 59 years, described his current ministry, "I answer Bible questions people put on my Facebook. Or I address messages sent to me through the mail and queries sent to me through e-mail. I continue to receive several questions each week from former students and from people who have read my books. My work is my hobby." (Stanley was born May 6, 1916, died July 12, 2014 at age 98.)

Beyond the writing of his books, former teaching assignments, and the visiting of 24 different countries, he spoke of his legacy, "I hope people will remember I always obeyed God. I prayed that He would help me do His will. As I interacted with students, I emphasized His faithfulness to me every day."

Doctor Horton spoke of his life-style, "We need to have an attitude of prayer throughout each day. I use my prayer language every day, sometimes more than once a day, in order to sense the presence of the Lord. I also work out in the MV Community Center exercise room for a half-hour, four or five days each week. And, I keep in touch regularly with my family here in Springfield and my two sisters in California."

Ninety-one-year-old Lillian Luckey lost two husbands, the first to a car accident and a heart attack, the second one to an ongoing heart problem and heart attack. Working in churches and assisting her second husband in Iowa and Missouri pastorates, she later began a volunteer ministry at MV in 1985. She taught Bible classes in the Manor for 14 years, and then moved into MV 12 years ago. (Lillian Luckey was born November 7, 1921, died March 27, 2016 at age 95.)

Her hobbies included reading and singing soprano in the MV choir. She gave up her teaching in the Manor because of a throat problem, which was later healed.

Her current ministry included visiting new MV residents. She assisted them in their settlement. Thus, she considered herself a "people person." Her prayer ministry began in pastorates years ago and continued as long as those people continued to call or contact her with their needs. Lillian participated in MV prayer groups, too.

She believes her legacy will be remembered, "as a person who expresses God's agape love through acts of service to residents at MV." Her ministry sometimes focused on grief recovery for those persons who had suffered the loss of a mate or a love one.

For Christians in their 60s, 70s, or 80s, she counseled, "Be sure Christ is Lord in your life. Ask Him to guide you. Maintain a right relationship with the Lord Jesus."

Lucille Freisen, age 92, and her husband John of 63 years, pastored for seven years, spent 33 years in A/G missions, primarily in Africa, and nine years in senior adult ministry in Kelso, Washington. They moved into MV in 2000.

She counseled, "A lot of what we accomplish in life has to do with attitude and our communication with the Lord. He has taught me I can live in peace. I talk to Jesus like He is my best friend, especially since John died in 2006."

Lucille reflected, "I'm upbeat by disposition and busy all the time. I can't play the piano, organ, saxophone, or sing anymore. However, I'm happy being a prayer warrior and an encourager to friends around me, and to those persons in several states with whom we became acquainted over the years."

"Plan for the future," she emphasized. "Life is a cycle. Plan ahead and the Lord will direct you."

The words of the hymn, *Work for the Night is Coming*, could be the theme song propelling forward the ministry of these nonagenarians. Jesus' words spoken in Luke 19:13 about the parable of the nobleman and his slaves, states a command obeyed by these saints—"Occupy 'til I come" (KJV).

In capsule summary, each person interviewed exhibits an enriched prayer life. Each individual interacts with their immediate and extended family members as well as the family of God. Each one has continued a hands-on ministry based upon their vocation of previous years. Each person looks up expectantly for his or her summons to heaven. All await Christ's soon return.

In days of loneliness, memories sustain. In moments of spiritual victory, prayers of gratitude ascend heavenward. In times of stress, the Word of God buoys the weary soul. Their example for us is clear. These seasoned veterans in the Lord's army have learned to laugh, love, lean on Jesus, and to bask in His presence.

8. THE STARS AND STRIPES FOREVER

(Written 2014)

INSTRUMENTALISTS, YOUNGSTERS WITH little experience, even seasoned professionals, thrill at the opportunity to perform one of John Philip Sousa's most popular marches, *The Stars and Stripes Forever*.

For me, that excitement occurred when I entered seventh grade. Both junior and senior high bands rehearsed together as one unit in my hometown of Payette, Idaho, a Class C school.

Our director, long-time music veteran, Jay Stoner began his career in band work before the 1900's. However, by 1932 both band and choral music participation became an accepted part of the public school curricula across America.

Addressed by his students as "Jay," he began directing bands in those early years in three different towns each day in Payette County – New Plymouth (1932-1939), Fruitland (1930-1959), and Payette (1930-1959).

In his last 29 years of public school music instruction, Jay directed only the band programs concurrently of the Fruitland and Payette schools. Altogether, Mr. Stoner taught music classes and directed bands for 76 of his 91 years.

Band Master Jay directed a summer county band in the Payette City Park every Thursday evening, which drew crowds of 2-4,000 plus people throughout the 20's, 30's, and 40's.

This venue continued with a move in the 50's to a new city park, complete with band shell. Mosquitoes and gnats, however, continued to be a problem, especially for vocalists.

I graduated from the University of Idaho in 1956, majoring in instrumental music. Before continuing my music education at the University of Michigan, I had the opportunity to direct the Payette County Band that summer in the new band shell.

We managed to pull together a few old-timers, some younger bandsmen, and a couple of band directors from nearby high schools in order to play the well-known marches and easily performed concert selections.

The family members of the bandsmen and other people milling around in the park, honked their car horns and applauded dutifully after each rendition, especially when we performed *The Stars and Stripes Forever*.

Before the advent of television, people flocked to their hometown city parks during the 20's to the 40's for band concerts, dramatic presentations, picnics, and social outings. After World War II, cultural interests changed with the introduction of television. The city park entertainment soon lost its glamour and crowd following.

Still today, when high school and college bands perform this well-known Sousa march, pulses beat faster, ears listen closely, mouths drop open in awe. Performers capture a person's attention by the rhapsodic flute phrases, the clarinet trills, the thrilling trumpet melodies, and those bombastic trombone and baritone lines, backed up with energetic tuba and Sousaphone huffing and puffing.

As a result of listening to the inspiring lines of *The Stars and Stripes Forever*, long-forgotten memories come to life and help us recall the traveling circuses, patriotic hometown parades, completed civic projects, Veteran's Day parades, community picnics, Fourth-of-July rodeos, Memorial Day commemorations, and a host of other activities that tell us, "We are a part of the grand United States of America."

May the Lord bless our country at all times, "the land of the free, and the home of the brave.

9. PASSAGE TO ETERNITY

(March 30, 2017)

A N OBSERVER OF AN older person lying in a hospital bed might consider this approaching near-death situation a gruesome stumbling block for that patient's future plans. However, it may lead to a glorious opportunity for the sick person to witness of his/her faith in Jesus.

The onlooker may interpret a patient hooked up to a maze of tubing as a scary scene. Both wait . . . wonder . . . aware of the body lying on the bed, wasting away. Each one wonders, when will resolution occur? The minutes fly by like the steady tic-toc of a pendulum in a standing wall-clock.

Visiting individuals as well as the patient pray in their own way: "God, will you do a miracle of healing today for all to see?" or, "Lord, please stop this intense misery?"

An attending nurse walks into the room filled with family members and close friends. She administers a dose of morphine to the infirmed one in hopes of reducing the increasing pain.

The conversation continues in hushed tones. The small group of concerned persons show signs of relief when the threshing of arms and twisting of the loved one's body lessen, then relax.

Some persons who receive hospice care at this point in their life may find themselves in that bed because of a shooting incident, or a malfunctioning heart issue, or a muscular disorder caused by an uncontrollable nervous system, or an unmanageable AIDS situation.

In this case, intestinal cancer created havoc. Depression, anxiety, and fear of death exacerbated this possible end-of-life drama.

Other caring friends come by during these days of frustration and helplessness to offer words of encouragement and their prayers for resolution that this extended period of suffering cease. Some visitors coming in, not experienced in making hospital visits, seem only able to utter observations about the changing weather patterns.

Some in the room can barely manage to mutter an attempted meaningful greeting. Nevertheless, most individuals proclaim words of hope, received by others present as a sign of respect for the terminally-ill patient. Thus, hope reigns as an eternal consequence for the gravely-ill friend.

During this waiting period, compatriots and kinsmen offer up more prayers for healing, even for a resolution of the illness. Appropriate Bible verses are quoted, others read, as the group gathers on each side of the bed, which sometimes rouses the loved one from sleep.

They realize the apparent resting person may look like a sleeping body, but can hear every spoken word of each conversation.

For those persons gathered together in the room, scripture verses voiced are meant to remind God of everyone's desire for a complete healing. For example, Exodus 15:26: "I am the LORD who heals you." (NKJV)

Psalm 103:1, 3 state: (v.1) "Bless the LORD, O my soul: And all that is within me, bless His Holy name! (v.3)) Who forgives all your iniquities, Who heals all your diseases." (NKJV)

Isaiah 53:3 says: "But He was wounded for our transgressions, He was bruised for our iniquities; The chastisement for our peace was upon Him, and by His stripes we are healed." (NKJV)

First Peter 2:24 states: "Who Himself bore our sins in His own body on the tree, that we, having died to sins, might live for righteousness—by whose stripes you were healed." (NKJV)

Matthew 4:23 tells us in the Sermon on the Mount that "Jesus went about all Galilee, teaching in the synagogues, preaching the gospel of the kingdom, and healing all kinds of sickness and all kinds of disease among the people." (NKJV)

While waiting for the Lord to respond, these verses caused some souls to review their own passage into eternity. Questioning themselves, "Am I prepared for this journey myself?"

Those questioning persons will discover that in heaven, there will be no itches to scratch, no pain to endure, no need for glasses to sharpen one's vision. The over-flowing power of Jesus' love will cancel out any presence of anger, hate, spitefulness, jealousy, envy, and a host of other inappropriate emotions or misguided actions.

Revelation 21:4 enumerates: "And God will wipe away every tear from their eyes; there shall be no more death, nor sorrow, nor crying; and there shall be no more pain, for the former things have passed away." (NKJV)

In that hospital room, the events of one day become lost in the activities of the next. The ever-present questions rise to the surface of everyone's thoughts at each visit: "Will this be the miracle day of healing?" Or, "Will this be the day our loved one graduates into eternity?"

On one occasion, a group of people assembled, and prayed for a definite response from God. Someone began to sing about the glory and love of the Lord. All joined in.

The Holy Spirit anointed each song. God's love permeated the atmosphere. Expectancy overwhelmed the small make-shift choir.

A repertoire of worship and praise songs filled the room. Memories of previous song fests caused the ensemble to render heart-warming choruses and hymns like "He Lives," "To God be the Glory," "Majesty," "Turn Your Eyes Upon Jesus," 'Give Thanks," and "He is Lord."

The serenade for the patient and the musical entreaty to Jesus brought into the patient's room the presence and power of the Holy Spirit.

No one rushed away. Each one singing felt the glorious presence of Jesus and the anointing of the Holy Spirit. Songs of thanksgiving soon filled the room. The worship and praise choruses satiated each being, bringing each person near Heaven's gates.

The group wanted no hindrances to their ardent pleas for a miracle. They voiced their requests in various ways: "How long, Lord, must this suffering go on? It's just going on, and on, and on."

"Please Lord, bring resolution one way or another! Her husband needs her."

Those on this prayer journey waited patiently . . . wondered expectantly . . . hoped every day with assurances from the Word. They knew God would move in His own time, in His own way, at His own speed, for His glory and majesty in order to manifest a miracle or bring about a resolution.

For the moment, they felt time ceased. Jesus' arms seemed to encircle each worshiper. Now, with the patient's next breath, surely resolution . . . .

They knew the person on the bed had accepted Jesus as Lord and Savior. Each participant knew their own eternity began at that moment they themselves had made a commitment to Jesus. They knew, also, the soul remains with the body until it ceases to function on earth. Then, union with Jesus transpires within the next nanosecond.

The Apostle Paul wrote about this moment in Second Corinthians 5:6-8, saying, when we are absent from the body, we will be present with Christ.

Friends waited expectantly for God's answer. His reply came early the next morning—home-going. Their loss signaled heaven's gain.

And so, another soul, this capable lady, called home by the Lord, shall receive a special award for her diligence in compassionate teaching, her faithfulness in living Christian values, and for her persistence in fulfilling daily duties and family responsibilities.

For this reason, those of us in her circle of friends shall praise the Lord Jesus every time our thoughts recall the good times we shared together with this cherished and loving soul—Ermalene.

10. VILLAGE LIFE IN MARANATHA

(March 10, 2017)

AMAZING PEOPLE LIVE in Maranatha Village, a long-time established Assembly of God retirement facility located in Springfield, Missouri.

Each resident could share a unique background of duty, dedication, and diplomacy from their life of service to humanity and their walk with the Lord. Approximately 500 people live at MV, another 100-plus persons work there either full- or part-time.

It seems every third day or so, a moving van or truck removes someone's household goods or unloads baggage for a new occupant or an incoming couple.

Campus activities provide various opportunities on a regular schedule for newcomers and residents to meet and interact with each other.

Occupancy may begin at 55 years of age. Most individuals or couples remain in MV until departing to heaven.

Although some residents move out voluntarily in their later years for various reasons.

For some, there may be financial constraints, or relatives may decide to provide palliative care for a loved one until his end of days. Whatever reason for the departure, it causes a significant change of residents over an eight-year period of time.

The clientele in MV can entertain a listener with awesome stories of events from their lives. Some accounts teem with sadness, others with anecdotes of happiness, a few tales seem downright unbelievable.

One person experienced losing a mate to cancer, another told of the jubilation of leading sinners to Christ, both at home and abroad. Some men speak of their long-term successful preaching ministries.

One veteran recalled the hurt of losing buddies during a war. One couple spoke of the joy found in their second marriage after surviving the pain of losing a first mate. A few speak of the loneliness of living by themselves for many years.

One couple walk hand-in-hand, and take long strolls during fair weather, sharing a new lease of God-anointed love. Each lost their first mate after several years of marriage.

They now enjoy the fulfillment of seeing their grown children leading successful lives and serving Christ. They adorn the MV campus with a lively, joyful attitude. Each one understands their Christian responsibilities and serve other persons for the glory of God.

One hard-working senior in his sixties, lost his wife recently due to illness. Depression plagued him for months. At a God-ordained time, a ninety-year-old lady caregiver entered the picture.

She counseled him over Saturday morning breakfasts at their favorite restaurant. His countenance gradually changed. Other factors aided his emotional healing. However, no one could take the place of the loss of both his first and later his second spouse.

Old age creeps up on seniors in the Village in unexpected ways. It may attack people by diminishing their eyesight, hindering their mobility, increasing their aches and pains, etc.

Leukemia wore down one man who enjoyed his Popsicle and dish of ice cream each day. Another man didn't realize the importance of good dietary habits; his overeating caused a heart problem and noticeable fatigue.

Later-life activity in a few MV seniors can best be described as unique. One ninety-year-old man continues to write textbooks for his former overseas students taught during an earlier missionary assignment.

One ninety-year-old lady painted various scenes at a large easel set up in her room. When you visit residents, you'll find one eighty-year-old lady whose walls display her vibrant paintings from an earlier period in her life.

Another lady remained active in the MV chapel choir until age 85, when her eyesight began to fail.

Some eighty-year-oldsters continue exercising by playing golf. A few octogenarians regularly play their musical instruments in the MV orchestra. And at least three ladies must have graduated from the Master Gardener program. The flowerbeds around their homes can only be described as exquisite.

Some seniors spend time each week in distributing items at a food bank for homeless people and low income persons. Several people walk around the campus and take time to visit with neighbors seen outside at their homes.

Early-bird walkers watch for turkeys, deer, geese, ducks, and other animals along their chosen morning or evening route.

The secret for longevity for most seniors—activity. More than one hundred persons volunteer their time, money, talent or assistance in some way to make living at Maranatha Village pleasant and inspiring for other occupants.

One retired grade-school teacher uses her talent in preparing attractive bulletin board displays. These delightful designs welcome residents who dine each day in the Community Center.

As some occupants begin to "downsize" the baggage in their homes, the Maranatha Village Mall (thrift shop) collects and resells bits and pieces and odds and ends.

The income from these sales has helped MV purchase additional equipment for the assisted living situations, staff, and persons in need of specific clothing or a health care item.

There are hazards to living in MV. Cars may zoom faster than the 15½ mile per hour speed limit and completely ignore the posted stop signs on campus. Life in MV is never dreary, seldom without incident, and usually directed to a higher spiritual plane.

In winter, an eerie silence can hover over snow-covered roofs. In spring, summer, and fall, however, activity abounds as many residents still consider themselves young-at-heart.

A periodic send-off funeral service highlights the passing-on to heaven of another soul called home by the Lord. It signals to others a life fulfilled, the great divide crossed over, another journey completed.

Thus, the community life-cycle continues in its preparation for each person to eventually transition to their eternal residency with Christ.

11. A DEAR NEIGHBOR AND BUD

(September 17, 2012)

HERE'S A GIFT FOR a man with a rod and a reel,
He buys his live bait in the store with fish meal.

This blanket gift he will feel in his chair a sure deal,

And drive to the lake with his golf cart and creel.

His wife cleans his catch in their bathtub, it's surreal.

She bangs on its head, with large pliers she peels.

Dear wife with sharp knife that she is, he just squeals.

She cleans and she cooks for his good house-keeping seal.

This gift shows a bait he might use, fish won't steal.

The Missus should buy him a boat for his zeal.

With bell he could peal, it would call even teal,

As fish in the pond often come near his heel.

Remember I say though the fish will not kneel,

Rev. Gerald might try a big net with his spiel.

It worked with his evangelism team when they prayed

healing for Filipinos.

All fish and all people are not dumb, our great God is their

keel.

So sleep well my Bud, use this gift's nice warm feel.

And cast until ice or cold waters congeal.

As always, we "shell" prevail,

God bless,

Charles

12. CREATED IN UNITY

Topic: Creation (August 23, 1988)

John 1:1-3. "Before anything else existed, there was Christ with God. He has always been alive and is Himself God. He created everything there is—nothing exists that He didn't make." (TLB)

JESUS PLACED THE STARS in the sky and the planets in rotation. The small grains along each shoreline are His handiwork as well as the multitudes who have walked those unending beaches. Every object in life has the stamp of the Almighty One upon it.

A star-apple fruit tree grew in our front yard in Metro Manila. It produced more fruit than any similar tree in our neighborhood. Its bent-over trunk and spacious arms produced large numbers of blossoms before its February harvest in the Philippines. The fruit bearing continued through most of March. The purple-skin covering enclosed a star-shaped delicacy fit for a king's table, which no one could have created except the Almighty God.

What life did Christ not create? Did He not fashion each leaf and branch of every star-apple tree? Its uplifted arms displayed individuality just as there are differences between you and me. This miracle of life helped us recognize Christ created every pebble and mountain, every minnow and whale, every crawling child and aging octogenarian. Christ's superiority becomes evident in every facet of life.

No one lives solely unto himself. Our Creator-Redeemer has fashioned us to fit together harmoniously. He desires we live together in unity.

PRAYER: Father, help us live in concert and in unity with one another in the harmonious manner our Creator has planned for each of us. In Jesus' name. Amen.

13. A RESURRECTED STUDY DESK

Topic: Holy Spirit (January 25, 1978)

John 15:26. "But when the Helper comes, whom I shall send to you from the Father, the Spirit of truth who proceeds from the Father, He will testify of Me" (NKJV).

S EVERAL YEARS AGO A neighbor gave me an old battered, wooden school desk for our second-grader. It was rough and dilapidated. It had been rained on several times.

It once had been a beautiful desk. Now as a discarded antique, it needed rehabilitation.

Sanding down all the defaced surfaces required extensive work. The wood drank up the stain and varnish as fast as I could apply it. Finally, it was ready to be placed in our home for use. But where?

Due to its large size, the only place available was near the front door. We set it partway into the living room and edging into our dining room. There in the center of busy family activities of each day, it fit best.

Our young one did much school work at that desk. It was a pleasant scene as our second grader conducted pretend projects in that crowded space. All of us were proud of its usefulness, even though it occupied an over-crowded area of our home.

Just as we refurbished that old desk, Jesus has taken us in hand and reclaimed us. As that old desk needed renovation, so does the soiled life of man need working on by the Holy Spirit, who remodels us for Christian service.

He sometimes scrapes, but gently refinishes our lives. Just as that reclaimed desk became the center of activity in our home, so Jesus the Master Carpenter places us in strategic areas for ministering daily. Being used by Him can produce much enjoyment, not only in our lives, but in the lives of others.

Kristian enjoyed that old desk. Similarly, when we give Jesus the Master Builder a chance to use us, we give Him great happiness. Friend, you may feel you've been discarded. You may think you're in poor shape. But the oil of the Holy Spirit comes to do more than just an "antique" job on each of us.

More than we can ever imagine, the Holy Spirit wants to restore us and "build us up" in Jesus.

PRAYER: Father, help me allow the great "Renovator," the Holy Spirit, to reconstruct and polish me. He can identify my needs better than I know them. Thank you, Lord. In Jesus' name. Amen.

14. WRITE JOHN, WRITE

Topic: Eternity (August 19, 1988)

Rev. 1:18. "I am He who lives, and was dead, and behold I am alive forevermore. Amen. And I have the keys of Hades and of Death" (NKJV).

W RITE SEVEN churches

Grace and peace to you from Him

Who is, was, will be!   Rev. 1:1-8

I, John, heard a voice

Someone like the Son of man

"Write on the Lord's Day!"   Rev. 1:10-13

Seven gold lamp stands

Paul's missionary churches

"Write those in Asia!"   Rev. 1:11-12

Seven angel stars

Guard, protect and minister .

All in His right hand!   Rev. 1:16, 20

His face shone brilliant

His voice sounded like rushing waters

"Write seven churches!"   Rev. 1:15-16

The First and the Last

He holds the keys for death and hell

He lives forever!   Rev. 1:17-18

"John, write what you see

Write what will take place later."

It shall be! Amen.   Rev. 1:7, 19

PRAYER: Lord, speak to me daily by your Word. Jesus help me listen and follow your prompting. Amen.

15. THE WAGES OF SIN BRINGS DEATH

Topic: Salvation (November 1976)

2 Corinthians 6:2. "Now is the accepted time; behold, now is the day of salvation" (NKJV).

THERE HAVE BEEN MANY beautiful scenes along the country side as I've traveled back and forth between Ellendale and Aberdeen these last two years while attending Trinity Bible Institute.

Sometimes flights of pheasants moved from field to hedge row cover, or ducks winged along the migratory route, or a precious baby lamb nursed in a nearby field.

One day I saw the mangled shape of a deer lying crumpled up in an irregular shape beside the road. This deer, apparently, had not seen the highway traffic.

At the last possible moment, it may have been blinded by headlights of an on-coming vehicle. For some reason, it did not move out of the way in time to escape being hit.

Some people are like that unfortunate deer. It was run over and knocked down on the busy highway. It shouldn't have been standing there.

Some persons have let a little sin into their lives, and woefully can't move away from it. Just like the vehicle that side-swiped that once beautiful animal, sin leaves its mark of destiny on a life.

The game warden or someone from the highway patrol must come and pick up the carcass and dispose of it. Many people today are lying crumpled up in an irregular shape beside the road of life.

When a person allows sin to come into his life, God—the game warden, has to eventually come and clean up the mess.

The deer on that highway may not have looked for traffic. Man often doesn't look for the consequences of sin. But both may receive the same reward: death.

Romans 6:23 says: "For the wages of sin is death, but the gift of God is eternal life in Christ Jesus our Lord" (NKJV).

I wished that gorgeous, four-footed creation of God would have stayed out of the way of just that one fateful car. Worse yet, I pray that man may not be side-swiped by one little sin gaining a foothold in his life.

PRAYER: Father, help me flee all unrighteousness and cling to You. Dear Lord, cause me to stay out of the byways of sin. Help me abide in Jesus and stay committed to Him! Amen.

16. FRAN'S BAKERY

Topic: The Bread of Life (May 1979)

John 6:51. Jesus said: "I am the living bread which came down from heaven. If anyone eats of this bread, he will live forever" (NKJV).

F RAN'S BAKERY IN ELLENDALE, ND makes very good bread and pastries. But these delicacies cannot compare with that exquisite Bread of Life, the Lord Jesus Christ.

Fran's bread, if not readily eaten, or properly taken care of, will become moldy after a few days.

Jesus the Living Bread, however, does not allow any mold to occur. This Living Bread cures anything which may show signs of rotting in one's life.

The difference between these two types of bread becomes apparent by the addition of a chemical preservative in the bread. Many commercial bakeries include this chemical preservative called calcium propionate or the chemical called BHA or BHT which retards spoilage.

For Jesus, the Living Bread, who came down from heaven, that special element is His Blood. Our Savior, the God-man Jesus, shed His Blood at Calvary for each of us, that we may be cleansed from leading sinful lives. With Jesus in our lives, we need not fear any spoilage.

As we participate together in a communion service, and partake in the eating and drinking of the elements, let's celebrate Jesus, Let Him, our Blessed Lord and Bread of Life, take out any "mold," any sin in our lives that may be trying to attach itself to us in any way.

Communion means we hold something together in common. It signifies a recognized partnership and an enjoyed fellowship.

In communion with Jesus, we can share in His resurrected life and in the power of our Lord and Savior. Communion provides fellowship with the Father, the Son, and the Holy Spirit.

PRAYER: Father, help me continue my Christian walk with Jesus, free from any "moldy" sinful encumbrances. Thank you, Lord. Amen.

17. THE SAFE SIDE OR THE SUICIDE

(June 13, 1983; *Clauser Newsletter*, September 1984)

TWO WARNINGS APPEAR on the rear mud flaps of several Filipino *jeepneys*: on the lower left, "Safe Side;" on the lower right, "Suicide." A small hand-painted, bright orange arrow points to either side of the vehicle one may choose for passing while driving.

The obvious message based on these visual warnings: "Will each one of us pass on the 'safe side' of life with Jesus?" To pass on the right side is a "No-No."

My morning drive from our Quezon City, Metro Manila, apartment to the Far East Advanced School of Theology normally took thirty-five minutes. Part of my route traversed the northern superhighway. Cars on this North Expressway sometimes passed a vehicle moving in the right lane by over-taking on the right shoulder.

This "suicide" action illustrates an impervious attitude toward the verities of life.

Acting impatiently, those drivers gave the impression of living only for the moment. Their actions and driving attitudes said: "Gangway, I'm coming through; I care only for myself." The time-shattering thought crossed my mind: "Are these drivers ready to pass on the 'safe side' of life with Jesus? Their eternity could begin in just seconds."

Man has but two basic choices in this short life: (1) accept Jesus and drive on the "safe side" or (2) choose to live in sin and place his name on the "suicide" list for eternity. One decision insures heaven; the other condemns to hell.

Paul admonished the centurion, shipmaster, and the owner (Acts 27:9-11), it would be "suicide" to continue sailing to Rome in the winter. Rather, it would be expedient and prudent to stay on the "safe side" and spend the bad sailing months at some seaside port. But those in charge would not listen to him.

The angel of God in Acts 27:24 told Paul: "Do not be afraid, Paul. You must be brought before Caesar" (NKJV). All 276 souls remained in the ship as directed. No life was lost.

Paul, by the Lord's leading, was able to take these souls around the "safe side." Had the superiors on board not listened to Paul, every soul might have been lost on the "suicide.

When it seems that a life might be broken apart by the violence of the waves of indifference, or stuck fast on a sandbar of indecision, or run aground on a rocky shoal of iniquity, let us remember: Jesus controls the storm and the direction it travels.

He becomes a fair haven for the needy, crying soul. Passing on the "safe side" demonstrates the desire of each caring heart. May each of us pass by on the "safe side" with Jesus, through the traffic decisions and moral actions of our lives.

18. THE BANANA THAT STRAYS FROM THE
BUNCH GETS PEELED

(June 1984)

THE EXTENSIVE FARMING OPERATIONS around General Santos City, Southern Mindanao, include coconut and banana plantations. I was able to observe first-hand the truth of bananas growing in a hand, upside down, and in a bunch. We were told Philippines farmers can grow sixteen different types of bananas.

I attribute the title for this story to Reverend Paul Davidson (circa 1975), one of my Bible instructors at Trinity Bible Institute. He and his wife Ava had been missionaries to China, but because of the Revolution there after WW II, transferred to the Philippines.

The Banana That Strays from the Bunch Gets Peeled describes his style of teaching. Christians must "hang" together in unity and purpose.

During the time of our teaching two block-session classes at the Assemblies of God Bible Institute of Mindanao the board chairman gave us a tour of his banana plantation.

Bananas, like other kinds of fruit, mature clustered tightly together. Christians, too, mature best in tightly knit groups. Jesus said in John 15:5: "Abide in me" that you "bear [bring forth] much fruit" (NKJV).

The growing process of a banana tree resembles Christian maturation. First, the farmer replants an old banana tree stump. This short seedling has been cut off near the ground. It looks ugly. But out of that decaying bulk pops a new stem. It soon becomes the trunk of a new banana tree.

As I watched two seasoned farm workers replant an old banana stump, it reminded me of how Jesus had been cut off in the prime of His ministry on earth.

He arose three days later in "newness of life" (Romans 6:4). Before long, the new banana sprout will rise up into a beautiful fruit-bearing tree.

We are coaxed and encouraged to attain new heights in our Christian maturity. Like that tender new trunk, Jesus wants us to become a productive fruit tree. Jesus said in Matthew 12:33: "A tree is known [recognized] by its fruit" (NKJV).

The harvested bananas were gauged, sized, and sorted by workers in a nearby packing plant. Similarly, God uses a "standards" gauge on each of us. "Measuring up" becomes His desire for each of us. Psalm 19:8 says: "The statutes of the Lord are right, rejoicing the heart" (NKJV).

However, a banana that strays from the bunch means a Christian may be bruised when there has been a lack of teaching and balanced doctrine in practical Christian living. "To be peeled" means we no longer have the Lord's protective covering.

Psalm 91:2 assures us: "He is my refuge and my fortress (v.4). His faithfulness [truth] will be your shield and rampart [buckler, bulwark]" (NIV).

Like each banana growing securely in a new stalk, we in Christ find continual care, security, and nourishment. In Him, the old stump, the old way of life, has become new life.

Don't let yourself become peeled apart by the problems of life, but live like good fruit. Good fruit grows best in bunches.

19. REDEEM THE TIME

Topic: Self-Discipline (April 7, 2015)

Ephesians 5:15-16 (NAS). "Be careful how you walk, not as unwise men, but as wise, (v.16) making the most of your time, because the days are evil."

Ephesians 5:15-16 (TLB). "Don't be fools; be wise: make the most of every opportunity you have for doing good."

THE HOLY SPIRIT URGES first-year students in Bible school, I learned first-hand, to "redeem the time." This constant encouragement to succeed for these kinds of students involves the learning of new ministerial skills associated with persistent prayer, in-depth Bible study, and ministry to people in need.

After completing four music degrees, I went to Bible school at age 40. In music school I learned to enter an instrumental practice room and not come out until I mastered my assignment for the next weekly lesson. In my Bible school studies, I applied similar principles in order to "redeem the time."

This same type of music school discipline helped me master Bible school ministries of prayer, Bible study, and effective communication.

It allowed me to endure my first assignment of nursing home ministry amid the unpleasant smells and the culture of older people living out their final years. Oral and written communication with these individuals also provided another key to successful relationships.

Whether a person finds himself a student or graduate, man or woman, single or married, dad or mom, grandpa or grandma, the Holy Spirit hovers over each of us and broods around us like a mother hen caring for her new-born chicks.

He nudges us to "redeem the time." Will you let Him gently encourage and lead you daily, to exercise the best response for each opportunity available in your life?

Dear Lord, may we "redeem the time" each day in order to take advantage of service opportunities for our family members, friends, and neighbors as You lead our humble efforts. May our every response glorify Your majesty. In Jesus' name. Amen

III. EPIC EVENTS ENCOUNTERED

1. A BULL IN OUR BACKYARD

(1944)

ACROSS THE MAJOR NORTH-SOUTH highway in front of our farm home, our neighbor Ollie prodded his prize Jersey bull down the lane at the edge of his hay field adjacent to my Grandpa's barnyard.

Like most ten-year-old boys that develop a certain amount of ability in performing barnyard chores, I felt inclined to show off my emerging strength by standing tall in our driveway, small stick in hand.

The excited bull snorted in anticipation of servicing a cow some 300 yards further down the highway at a neighbor's corral. I had never seen such a large critter, especially one snorting, stamping the ground, and looking around for that bovine partner.

I bravely stood in our gravel driveway, ready to assist Ollie and keep the bull from entering our property. Ollie, I knew, planned to enter the highway about fifty feet from our front yard.

The bull, however, raised its head, looked my way and ran away from Ollie. It started to charge and chased me. Somehow, I exhibited enough sense to instantly drop my switch and run as fast as my little legs could propel me to the back door of our home, about forty feet away.

With heart pounding rapidly and my leg muscles throbbing with pain, my lungs gasped for air. I jumped up the back door steps, two at a time and dashed inside the screen door of our porch. At that moment, that red-eyed hulk climbed up the top step, but stopped outside the screen door.

I think Ollie ran faster than the bull. He arrived immediately, tied a rope around the bull's neck, placed a clamp in its nose, and led it away for its intended purpose

I didn't know Jesus yet. But His protective arms knew me!

2. MY WHIZZER MOTORBIKE

(2014)

Several of us fourteen-year-old kids in my hometown begged our parents for a bike to ride to high school. Dad bought me an old relic, welded together, which needed a paint job.

Happy for a bike, but ashamed of its condition, my embarrassment soon ended. The ugly-looking contraption of rusted pipes separated into two halves within ten days, completely beyond repair.

I grew up on a little acreage in central Idaho, and at this time in my life, Dad gave me a young Jersey heifer to care for. Within one year, as one of the five cows in our small herd, Blue Eyes started producing milk.

Dad also provided a can for me to send the milk to the local creamery. My first pay check: $4.37.

Dad banked those precious dollars each week which I received from my business enterprise. In a few months, I pestered my parents to buy me a Montgomery Ward bicycle, one which came with post-World War II, heavy-duty, balloon-like tires.

At last, they agreed. Like many of the guys my age, I also wanted a motor mounted on my two-wheeler.

Meanwhile, my faithful Blue Eyes kept producing milk, which helped me accumulate more dollars. So, with $108 in savings, Dad and Mom gave me permission to purchase a Whizzer motor for the Montgomery Ward bike.

Boy, oh boy! Now I could ride with the pack – that is, with the other freshmen who drove motorbikes. My first motorized wheels, wow!

North of our home, a small incline raised the contour of the state road which ran in front of our farm. With no traffic on the horizon, I could coax my Whizzer up to maximum speed, zoom down the slope.

I attained 60 miles an hour on windless days, the maximum speed allowed on this major, north-south highway. What an exciting half-mile ride!

Except, one day as I sped past our home and immediately started to turn into my Grandpa's driveway near our home, the motorbike fell sideways under me and slide a few feet on the asphalt topping.

Because at that speed I turned too abruptly. Immediately I looked to my left for oncoming traffic behind myself. Praise the Lord, no cars or trucks in sight!

With only a skinned knee, but with dampened enthusiasm and a sudden loss of pride, I learned a valuable lesson: Consider the consequences. When you drive, don't speed! Your life may hang in the balance.

3. AN UNEXPECTED MOUNTAIN RACE

(2013)

THE GRACEFUL DOE began to run frantically beside us, trying to escape the overpowering roar of Dad's pickup motor. To her right, stood a high, five-strand, barb-wire fence.

To her left, thundered our dust-covered vehicle loaded with tarp-covered fishing gear, camping equipment, and sleeping bags. A dust-cloud rose ominously on the gravel road behind us which may have scared the animal and prevented its slowing down.

Dad took me camping and fishing on most weekends during the summer after my sixth grade. We traveled to different locations in the mountains of central Idaho on each outing.

Some weekends, we stream fished with fly poles. Other weekends, we trolled on a lake with Dad's World War II rubber boat.

Each excursion provided me an exposure to historical sites, new scenery and exiting experiences. On this trip, we suddenly found ourselves beside a magnificent deer, grazing and walking in the grass beside our rocky road.

Dad quickly placed his pipe in the ash tray and held on to the steering wheel with both hands, not knowing what to expect.

I picked up my baby Brownie camera, ready for a memorable nature shot. I thought, *What might that deer do next? I better take a couple of pictures before that gorgeous animal might change course and disappear.*

The speedometer indicated 25 miles per hour. Dad accelerated to 30 so the animal wouldn't try to jump across the road in front of us to escape into the meadow on our left. If that happened, that beautiful creature could cause an accident in an attempt to evade us.

Dad increased the truck speed to 35; the deer similarly increased its stride and pace. With tongue hanging out, the quadruped increased its race beside us to 45 miles per hour.

A steep mountainside adjacent to the right side of the wire fence kept the fleet-footed Olympian from attempting to escape by jumping over the razor-sharp barrier.

How would the race end? No other vehicles were in sight as we continued side by side in this uncanny race. The mountain valley began to narrow as we started a slow climb through a tumbleweed-congested arroyo. Now at 55 miles per hour, who might give up first? Who might win the race?

My heart pounded in my chest like those pebbles that buffeted the underside of Dad's pickup. I wondered, *How long will this exhausted deer continue running before it drops?*

Soon, the hillside and barb-wire fence made an abrupt turn to the right. The gasping animal turned immediately and followed the fence line.

Knowingly, the gazelle-like runner, sensed the race terminated, felt the danger was past, and slowed its pace. The doe, I'm sure, searched for a nearby creek and a refreshing drink of water. It had been as frightened in this unexpected race as we had been amazed at finding ourselves in the unusual encounter.

The desert road meandered to the left, which caused us to slow down and discontinue the race. However, both runners, the doe and the pickup, clocked out at 58 miles per hour at this imaginary finish line.

The duration of the race -- would you believe it? – I guessed not more than three minutes.

We parked at a turnout to catch our breath and relax from the tension of this extraordinary confrontation. I asked Dad, as my racing pulse returned to normal, "May I have a sandwich?"

"Yes. I'm ready, also, for a bite to eat and a drink of water."

"What do you think Mom will say about that deer racing beside us?"

"She will probably scold me for driving fast on a mountain road, and say, 'No chocolate cake for either of you boys for a whole week.'"

"Well, we just wanted to see how fast that deer could run. Dad, I think we better catch a whole wash tub full of trout for Mom."

"Yes, and Bud, we should tell her, we missed her fine cooking.

4. OUR THREE-LEGGED WONDER DOG

(1968)

M Y WIFE, MARY, LOVES dogs—small, medium, large-sized, brown, black, mixed color, collie, Dalmatian, terrier, dachshund, Sheltie, Heinz 57 variety, or any mutt that can catch her attention and desires to be petted.

For example, when we watch the noon edition of Springfield KY3 News, the animal shelter from north Springfield will often feature three or four dogs ready for adoption. Mary will "ooh" and "aah" over each animal presented that needs a home.

Earlier in our marriage, we lived in Beatrice, Nebraska (pronounced be-AT-rice by Nebraskans). One Saturday morning as I drove out to the local airport for my flying lesson, the manager asked me if I would like to take home a new-born puppy. An itinerant mother had delivered her litter of pups behind the repair hanger.

Later at lunch, I told Mary about the five, cute, part-poodle puppies with eyes now opened. I made a passing observation and thought nothing more of our conversation.

You know, just doing my part to communicate well with my wife. I wanted to keep her informed of current events and keep up good communication for my part of our marriage.

But within two hours, unbeknown to me, she went to the airport repair hanger, surveyed the litter, played with each one, and made a decision to bring home the cuddly white female which displayed the best manners as it interacted with its siblings. Soon, I heard our backdoor bell ring.

There stood Mary, smiling and meekly looking up at me with a determined look in her eyes, holding both hands full of the wiggly four-legged canine close to her face, while it yelped for something to eat. With a most submissive look on her face, she pleaded, "May we come in?"

How could I say, "no." She caught me off guard. I admit, I felt ready for a dog, too. We called her "Mimi," after the female lead in Puccini's opera, *La Bohème*, because she was part French poodle.

Her father a black French poodle, her mother a Heinz 57 kind of dog. Mimi endeared herself to our household for fifteen years.

Our infant daughter, Cindy, arrived a few months later in 1968. Fortunately, both became good friends. However, during that adjustment period, Mimi would often place her paw on Mary's leg, as if to say, "Don't forget me. I'm here, too."

Cindy, at age 1½, decided she wanted to know more about Mimi's long-haired coat. She thought, "I like the feel of that soft white fluffy stuff." Mimi, lying on the floor near Cindy and Mary, yelped when Cindy tried to yank out a handful of Mimi's coat.

Mimi, in self-defense, turned to Cindy and nipped at her hand. Mary quickly separated the two, patted a spank on both, and spoke sternly. Both realized the error of their action, but after a few hours separation, their friendship resumed.

I exercise before beginning my activities for each day. One morning when I ran in place in the corridor of our home, Mimi came to watch me.

As I continued a few more repetitions, she looked at me sidewise, cocked her head to the right, then to the left, as if to ask, "What in the world are you doing? You are not going anywhere?"

Not understanding my leg motions, she considered this activity a strange event. She started to bark in a low voice. This questioning growl accompanied a pretend nipping at my toes.

As a teachable pet, I knew she wanted to join me in whatever new trick might come forth through what she considered silly hand and feet motions. The best response I could produce for our smart canine—a stomping of my feet and a verbal command, "Go get your ball!"

She understood that request and promptly searched our living room for her baseball size rubber ball with a small metal bell tucked inside its thick exterior.

Within moments, her quivering nose discovered its location. She returned it to me, triumphant with tail wagging, head held high, ready again to play "catch."

I remember once in 1970, we began packing our car in McCook, Nebraska and prepared to depart for a vacation. Both Mimi and Cindy, now almost three years old, howled and cried until we set up the playpen in the flattened back seat area of our station wagon, placed Cindy inside her play area and Mimi on her blanket, both side by side.

The pandemonium stopped and we continued loading our suitcases and travel gear in the back of the vehicle.

We lived in Aberdeen, South Dakota, 1973-1976. A neighborhood city park located three blocks from our home gave us opportunities to walk Mimi and teach her to ride a small merry-go-round, to slide down an elementary school type slide, and coax her to walk on the open, half-shell monkey bars apparatus with our close assistance.

She exhibited excitement, great patience, and obedience for this exercise. Thus, I believe she could have been trained successfully as a circus dog.

In those seven years we lived first in Aberdeen, SD and then in Ellendale, ND, we would spend our Christmas and summer vacation times alternating between my parent's home in Payette, ID and Mary's parent's home in Marion, MI.

On those trips when we would arrive in Mary's hometown, Mimi awoke from her hibernating position in the back seat of our car.

She grew restless, emitted a low bark and whine. Somehow she knew we would soon arrive at grandpa and grandma's home, our destination a few blocks ahead.

Especially, when we drove up the hill for the last two blocks her enthusiasm came unleashed. Mary's parents gave special attention to Mimi and let her stay inside their home. Mimi remembered previous visits and knew they loved her.

One time in Aberdeen we had gone grocery shopping and left her in our home. Usually, we left a shade partway up at a south window so she could stand on the davenport, rest her paws on its back in order to look out the window, and see people going by or traffic passing through the street.

For some reason, we didn't do it that time. When we returned we couldn't find Mimi for a few minutes. Finally, she came into view, crouched down before us, fearful of reprisal.

Then we noticed scratches on the end table by the west porch area. We knew immediately she had gone there to observe outside activity since the shade had not been raised.

We realized she had tried to stand on this table which had a revolving top. It had spun around as she attempted to look westward toward the porch. Then, she accidently fell down in her attempt to see outside and scratched the table top in trying to maintain her balance.

We knew from her actions she felt ashamed. It took a little while to assure her all was okay. We later used a furniture coloring pencil to repair the damage as best possible. From then on, we remembered to raise the shade on the south window whenever we left home for errands about town.

I took Mimi with me whenever I needed to drive to the post office, gas station or engage in other quick errands. Her assigned position—the back seat of the car. She barked with excitement over any possibility of a car ride.

Whenever I re-entered our car after completing each errand along the way, she stood on the back seat with paws on top of the front seat close to my back, and licked the back of my right ear lobe.

I tolerated the tickling and wet sponge effect for about three or four swipes, then leaned forward out of her reach. I gently said, "Sit down, Mimi." Each time I wondered, "Is this an act of love and devotion on her part?" or "Does she find salt there from my perspiration?"

I did shower every day. Perhaps she enjoyed my after-shave lotion. I decided Mimi showed her affection as a typical dog, with many licks given in friendship.

Mary and I often stopped by an ice cream parlor after completing business excursions around town. Mimi as usual rode in the back seat on these outings. When we ordered ice cream cones and sat in our car to relish the treat, we would remember to save the last part, the tip at the bottom of the cone with a few beads of our favorite flavors for Mimi.

With tail wagging, she consumed each offering in one wide-mouth gulp, which signaled her appreciation of the dessert. A lick or two behind my right ear and a swish of her tongue across Mary's hand indicated her readiness for more of the same delicacy.

Another time in Aberdeen, we left Mimi with a church acquaintance while we departed for a two-week vacation. Upon our return to our friend's home, we found Mimi had only three legs—her right rear leg amputated.

The helpful lady had somehow left her front door ajar. Mimi escaped, but got hit in traffic on her way back to our home.

A kind policeman who knew we would want the dog cared for, saw our name on one of Mimi's dog tags and the veterinarian's name on the other.

For that reason, the vacation became expensive. Since the accident happened shortly after we left town, Mimi had about ten days to recover before we returned.

Upon our return, she perked up at our presence and came limping across the living room floor to greet us. Then she attempted to lick our cheeks and hands profusely as we gave her hugs and encouragement for success in her new walking style.

Mimi convalesced during her first few days at home. We could tell the accident had taken a heavy toll on our little dog. We did not encourage any strenuous play activity for about three weeks, like running after her ball or trying to catch it in the air. We carefully assessed her endurance in each period of play.

By God's grace, she grew stronger each day and her good left leg soon supported her body motions well. Walking on three legs did not hinder her ability to maneuver. In time, she moved almost as fast on her three legs as before the accident with four.

The veterinarian had done a masterful job in removing her crushed right leg. We had two flights of steps in our Aberdeen home. As Mimi recovered, we encouraged her one day to attempt to climb these stairs. I remember Mary, our daughter Cindy, and me, encouraging Mimi on the last three steps in her climb to the top.

We could see her determination to succeed, her desire to please us, and her back leg trembling. We cheered loudly, clapped our hands, and hugged her upon completion of the difficult feat. She, of course, expressed her happiness with more tongue licks on our cheeks and hands.

Had she spoken, we would have heard, "I did it! I climbed the stairs!" Yes, pets can give their owners pleasure, but owners can give their pets comfort and joy, too.

I attended Trinity Bible Institute in Ellendale, ND, 1974-1980, taught classes and worked in administration. Occasionally, I would stretch out on one end of the davenport in our home after lunch.

Mimi would jump up and occupy the other end. We snoozed together. Also, whenever I would mow the grass or shovel snow at our Ellendale home, She expected to "help" and be close by me.

Mimi loved to play "catch," whether with her rubber ball and embedded bell, a Frisbee in the back yard, or a soft snowball after a winter storm. She enjoyed crunching a mouthful of that compacted white stuff.

But when I clipped her long hair in the summer months, she would endure with patience, because she knew a trip to the bathtub followed, after which she would run around inside our home at full speed releasing her pent-up energy.

Christmas was a special time for all of us. In Ellendale, we wrapped a rubber ball with bell inside for Mimi's Christmas gift. For at least three Christmases we enjoyed her reactions.

She would hear the bell as we laid the gift down on the floor. Immediately, she would go to work tearing off the wrapping paper with her teeth while holding the package between her two paws in order to gain access to the rubber ball with its bell.

Afterward, we encouraged and petted her. It was truly a family event. She loved to play with that rubber ball and would bring it to us to throw for her to receive, sometimes straight to her mouth as she stood only a few feet away, at times a toss to the other side of the room, other times a fast roll-away on the floor.

Mimi understood our commands. Whether we said, "Find your ball," or "Get your bone," or "Bring your collar." She never made a mistake. However, during times of blizzards in Ellendale, she let it be known at night when she needed to go outside. Mary would take her to the back door where Mimi had to be pushed out by Mary's foot in order to make her go outside to do her business. Mary spoke, "YOU woke me up, OUT you go!"

Our trips to the Vet's office in Ellendale caused stress for Mimi. We traveled about one mile down a graveled road outside of town to make our annual doggie visit for heart worm and other shots.

Mimi knew as soon as we turned off the highway, where we were headed. She began to quiver and cuddled up against Mary, even whimpering.

For our part, it appeared comical to see her fearful reaction, but we knew she had experienced trauma from the car accident. The memory of the removal of her leg had not been forgotten.

Upon leaving the Ellendale Vet's office, her countenance changed with an abundance of tail wagging and more tongue licking of hands and cheeks. After this ordeal each year, we stopped by the ice cream parlor for cones.

We itinerated (visited our denominational churches to enlist prayer and financial support, 1980-1982) in preparation for missionary ministry in the Philippines. Thus, Mimi became a permanent house guest and constant companion for Mary's parents.

Whenever her father drove around their small, north-central Michigan town to do errands, she "accompanied" him for his stops at the post office, gas station, coffee shop, and elsewhere.

But arthritis took a heavy toll on Mimi during the last two years of her life. The pain caused her to turn around five or six times, first one way then the other, before she could plop down on her blanket at night beside Mary's mother's side of the bed.

Within a week after we left for the Philippines, Mary's dad assumed the difficult responsibility to engage the Vet's assistance to put Mimi down because of this illness and other old -age problems which she suffered.

Epilogue

During our itineration, we met other adorable and talented canines. I remember a black terrier that lived in Cody, Wyoming, who on command to pray, would sit up, put its two front paws together and assume an attitude of prayer, at which time it would howl long and sorrowfully. Of course, it expected a treat afterward from its owners.

Another dog, a medium-sized black mutt that lived in Michigan, loved to sing by the piano while assuming that prayerful attitude of sitting up on its hind legs.

This pooch showed off his tenor voice with enthusiasm while joining the Bible study group as they sang praises and worshipped the Lord.

I recall a third dog, a medium-sized dachshund that resided in Shoshone, Idaho. Herbie thought he was a person. His joy overflowed at greeting guests. Herbie lived in the parsonage, outfitted with an extra-large and long living room used for conducting Bible studies and entertaining guests.

A davenport had been placed at each end of the room. A sizable coffee table occupied the center area between the two sofas.

Herbie loved to run from one davenport to the other by jumping up on one arm, running across the back of the sofa, down the other arm, then racing to the other davenport to perform the same gymnastic feat.

In our presence, he traversed this circular path four times in quick order before stopping to catch his breath. It was an unusual display of agility and endurance.

I grew up in central Idaho. We had four different dogs during the time I attended public school. Three were killed in traffic while attempting to cross the major highway in front of our rural farm home. A fourth had to be placed in another home 35 miles away because of his bad habit of eating the dog food set out at our various neighbor's homes for their own four-legged friends.

This loss left a depressed attitude in my mind about the prospect of keeping a dog in our home, especially during the first six years of our marriage—until Mimi came into our lives. She gave us great joy and love.

After 40 years without her, we still have vivid memories of that canine's heart-warming companionship. Jesus, indeed, blessed our family when he sent us Mimi, who in her mid-life, became our three-legged wonder dog

5. AN AMERICAN-STYLE THANKSGIVING CELEBRATED WITH FILIPINO FRIENDS

(1997. The dialogue portions of this essay have been reconstructed, the content is factual.)

DON'T DO IT AGAIN without the proper documentation!" The customs inspector at the Metro Manila airport inquired about the dampness around the metal-band edges of missionary Ty's open suitcases.

"You must have a meat permit to bring these birds into the Philippines."

However, after a prolonged explanation concerning the unusual transport and the importance of celebrating the American Thanksgiving, The official waved our courier through without penalty.

Three frozen turkeys wrapped in newspapers and towels lay hidden in his luggage on the flight from Guam to Metro Manila. Filipino restaurants seldom offer turkey on their menus.

Thus, Thanksgiving Day preparations began early in the morning on November 27, 1997, at the Asia Pacific Theological Seminary, located on a step hillside in the city of Baguio, Northern Luzon, Philippines.

"Leota," Mary said, breathing rapidly, "both our ovens down the hill registered 350 degrees." She slumped down in a chair because of the steep climb back up to her friend's home.

"Each turkey sizzled as I pulled aside the aluminum foil for a quick peek. The thermometer in each bird confirmed our roasting plan continues on schedule."

"My oven performed well, too," Leota replied. With hands on her hips, she looked toward her house keeper, and reviewed her final instructions for making dressing and baking the last of seven assorted pies. Then she checked the temperature gauge in her turkey.

All the while she continued her non-stop dialogue, "This turkey has started to turn brown. We should check the other ovens once more to see that the meat does not become overdone. 'Lord please, no roasting disasters today.' And Mary, you make the gravy."

"Oh no, not me! I've been known to have dumplings in my gravy. However, if you insist, I'll try."

"Umm, please check your two ovens once more at the missionary homes before you start the process." Leota checked her wrist watch three times in nervous anticipation of completing her part of the dinner arrangements.

"By then, I'll send our two yardmen to bring the birds up to the dining room kitchen at the Student Center and we can begin the preliminaries for our celebration.

"I think, however, our missionaries and guests have already started by drinking coffee." Then, with a wink of her eye, she jokingly said, "Mary, write it in your diary. We shall call ourselves the 'Turkey Patrol.'"

"I'm on my way," Mary exclaimed. The screen door squawked behind her as it slammed shut.

Leota muttered in disgust, "I must call maintenance tomorrow and make sure their man fixes my problem with that noisy door. It embarrasses me every time a friend or student comes to visit."

The problem for Leota, the head cook for our celebration—find enough ovens in faculty homes on campus in which to roast the birds. The Lord, never late, provided for that necessity.

Leota and Mary, ever vigilant, had worked up their appetites by walking up and down the steep hillside to missionary homes where they checked on the roasting activity. The birds roasted well and the holiday dinner set-up and food preparations progressed with few hindrances.

Mary wrote in her diary about the activities of the day. "Leota and I decorated the tables in the Student Center. The room looks pretty. About 3:00 p.m. things began to get hectic.

"We had to put pickles and cranberry sauce in dishes, place salt shakers, sugar bowls, etc., on a tray.

"About 3:30 p.m., a staff member began slicing turkeys. He continued until about 5:00 p.m. As turkeys were removed from pans, the juices were brought to Leota's home."

Mary prayed and began to make the gravy. I stirred and prayed that it would taste good, then thanked the Lord for the right consistency.

We served about 41 people, including the six speakers and their wives who were here for the 50th anniversary of the Tuding Assembly of God, located down the hill east, a short distance from Baguio."

We began our festivities by singing the regular seasonal songs: *"We gather together to ask the Lord's blessing . . . Sing praises to His name, He forgets not His own,"* and *"Come, ye thankful people come, raise the song of harvest home; All is safely gathered in."*

Before our feast, one of our senior missionaries offered a Thanksgiving prayer. Charles later recalled, "Such a bountiful buffet! The harvest trimmings and food would make our Puritan forefathers approve the feast. It reminded Mary of past prayers and meals at churches we visited during our itineration times.

"But as we sat down for this harvest dinner, the rich presence of the Lord permeated each conversation while mountains of food disappeared into hungry mouths of those persons seated around us."

Leota remarked, "We continued throughout the afternoon to celebrate this glorious event by singing more songs. We enjoyed abundant fellowship, ate pumpkin pie and walnut pie topped with whipped cream and honey, and even consumed generous portions of chocolate cake with vanilla ice cream.

"A European monarch could not have taken delight in a more delicious meal."

As the afternoon and evening activities began after the meal, some couples played rook, battleship, monopoly, or other games. Some people sat around trading stories, drinking large amounts of coffee or tea, during which time everyone devoured the last mouthfuls of their favorite cookies, pie, and/or ice cream.

The younger set texted their family in the States or their friends at Faith Academy, the missionary children's school in Metro Manila.

Thus, our time together for the observance of this important American holiday, became a family affair, similar to the Filipino extended family gatherings of 100 or more close-knit relatives.

Except in our missionary families, the children call the adults, other than their own parents, by the affectionate names of either "aunt" or "uncle."

For those parents with small numbers of their own children, this designation builds esteem in the adult recipient. This extended, informal family relationship continues for years, even

233

after the missionary family leaves their field of service, retires, or moves to another assignment.

Mary's diary for this day concludes with these thoughts. "I was so tired tonight, I was ready to drop. Two turkeys would have been sufficient for our get-together. After the clean-up, we all sat around and talked awhile in Leota's home in order to wind down and relax."

Unmeasured time, leisure, and tranquility marked this banquet as an extraordinary day of remembrance for commemorating the founders of our country.

6. THE RED SEA CROSSING

(February 16, 2015)

"MOSES, LIFT UP YOUR ROD . . . stretch out your hand over the sea . . . divide it" (Exodus 14:16).

Moses knew that voice of authority. "Yes, LORD. I thank and praise You for creating an escape route for Your people."

Throughout the afternoon mixed emotions surfaced in people's hearts. First, unbelief grew rampant that the Egyptian army would pursue the fleeing Jewish nation.

Fear of a quick assault caused disgust with Moses and hatred of his leadership. Questions of survival and thoughts of possible extermination exploded in the minds of many persons.

"Do not be afraid," Moses declared. "Stand still, and see the salvation of the LORD" (Exodus 14:13). "The LORD shall fight for you, and you shall hold your peace" (Exodus 14:14).

Then, the impossible happened. Undulating swells of sea water collided with tongues of crashing waves. The crests fell and slapped the ocean floor repeatedly. Mud puddles dried up. Sand piles blew flat. Pools of minnows and small fish flapped sideways into the darkness of the nearby turbulent walls. Jagged rock surfaces fell smooth in the face of the high-speed east wind.

Suddenly, "dry ground" (Exodus 14:16).

"Move along, my brothers ("baa-baa," sheep bleated nervously.) Stay in line, people. Aaron, take the lead" ("ee-yaaw-eeyaaw," donkeys stomped the ground.).

"Joshua," Moses urged, his hands beating the air and motioning like a rush-hour traffic cop, "walk the tribes as fast as our little ones can pace themselves. Run, when possible.

"Folks, we must hurry through this crossing God pro-vided for us" ("moo-moo," the cows wondered why the delay in their regular milking schedule.).

The frustrated band of almost two million exhausted travelers edged themselves and their frightened animals down into the narrow trough provided by the rolled-back water. They walked cautiously, but determinedly, through the cascading mountains in order to elude the armed threat directly behind their line-of-march.

All night long, the cloud of fire lighted their way to safety, while on the other side of the cloud, a pillar of darkness stalled and isolated the Egyptian charioteers and horsemen.

The aged leader of the young Israelite nation felt certain death awaited the unbeliever trudging into the tunnel of white-caps. He prayed non-Jews migrating with them would learn the Jewish way of life and accept the leadership of their LORD God.

"Merciful God," Moses pleaded, "please send Your Spirit to help the widow, the orphan, the weak, our strong young men and their loved ones. All our families need Your assistance and guidance."

After Moses' prayer, he heard a young boy call for help. "Uncle Josh," the little voice squeaked, "will you help me, please, with my broken sandal lace? I don't know what to do. I can't fix it."

"Sure, Sam. Climb up on my back. I'll repair it as soon as we climb out the other side of this walkway."

Moses knew the LORD exercised patience with the Is-raelites at the moment, because the light continued to glow, the dry ground remained firm, and the towering walls of water did not crumble.

In that passageway of deliverance, each family accepted their leader's instructions. Obedience prevailed because of their previous military training. "The children of Israel went up in orderly ranks out of the land of Egypt" (Exodus 13:18). This discipline and their faith, began its development in the land of Goshen.

Meanwhile, Moses maintained his command post on the rock pinnacle. With eyes kept open, he praised the great I-Am-that-I-Am, the Creator of heaven and earth. "LORD, if I thank you a thousand times, it would never be sufficient to express our gratitude for Your protection and deliverance."

The next morning, perhaps twelve to fifteen hours after the escapees entered the passageway and successfully emerged, the LORD told Moses: "Stretch your hand over the sea, that the waters may come back upon the Egyptians" (Exodus 14:26).

The result: A watery "death to all the army of Pharaoh that came into the sea after them" [the Israelites] (Exodus 14:28). (It is presumed Pharaoh died also in the water.)

People acclaimed in the aftermath:

"I trust Moses."

"Moses will obtain the LORD's help for us when we need it."

"I don't want to cross swords with our God."

"We better shape up, we're headed to the Promised Land."

"What an amazing God, so helpful, so capable, so lov-ing."

"I believe in the LORD God, Almighty. He's real!"

7. SQUADRONS OF AIRPLANES

(Summer 1943)

OVERHEAD CAME THE deafening roar without warning of airplane engines, displacing the peacefulness of our small farm community, Payette, Idaho.

Thousands of warplanes, an enormous collection of bombers, transport aircraft, and fighter planes, passed overhead on their way to Seattle in preparation for departure to the Pacific Theater operations of World War (WW) II.

One squadron, then another—too many to count, passed low overhead. Perhaps at no more than 3,000 feet, the spectacle sounded like a plague of angry hornets.

At first, I thought it a an invasion of wasps or bumble-bees or crickets or grasshoppers. At nine years of age, I was playing in the backyard of our farm home.

We learned this gigantic flight armada had assembled at the Mountain Home Air Base in central Idaho for this leg of their trip. Like migrating geese and ducks, but instead, birds of war.

This gargantuan covey, snarled out-of-tune with a deafening roar foreboding trouble, had organized for a different purpose.

These metal ornithological creatures droned powerfully in the sky above us, never changing position or bearing. Their destination predetermined, their resolve established. Success of this mission heralded as a foregone conclusion.

This vivid memory as a nine-year-old boy returned in later years, every time I saw migrating geese. Both the geese and the planes, represented to me the pride, power, and purpose of the United States of America.

Both groups were guided by God's hand. Both entities shared in the history making of our mighty nation. The hand of God provided the geese as a provision of food, the planes an emblem of industrial might.

8. SNOW GEESE EN ROUTE SOUTH

(November 3, 2009)

THE NEWLY-HARVESTED CORNFIELD across Highway 30 North in front of our home, north of Payette, ID glistened with a momentary stop for the fluttering of migrating snow geese headed south.

I was eight years old in the late fall of the wartime year 1942.

Few cars traveled this road beside our small ten-acre farm during those years. Those graceful birds feasted undisturbed on the leftovers from Landowner Ollie's recent harvest.

Gazing for hours in wonderment through the large 4 X 8-foot plate glass window set in the east wall of our living room, we observed the hunger-ridden activities of those travel weary creatures.

Their unexpected stopover for feeding in our neighbor's field continued for two days. The Lord made sure no roaming dogs harassed those contented flocks.

The birds had arrived in droves, one flight after another, gracefully settling down in remaining open spaces, each elegant body sometimes side-slipping at the last moment to avoid collision with other honkers.

Adeptly spreading their feet for a short approach landing, each bird dropped down a short distance in free-fall to occupy a choice site.

Some geese would rise up periodically to reposition themselves among others amid the inviting, but crumpled and negligible remaining cornstalks.

This glorious event seemed to be a special one-time present from the Lord, arranged for our benefit since our home was not located on the regular migratory route of these birds.

We wondered how these hundreds of snow geese found any kernels of corn in the field.

Our neighbor had carefully gathered in his harvest. No stalks were left standing. However, his equipment had apparently spilled sufficient amounts of corn or left the edges of the field untouched, which encouraged the flooding invasion of migratory birds into this five-acre stubble field.

I shall never forget the sight of those bold white-colored avian creatures providing an exciting motion picture of grace and splendor against the drab fall background of a harvested, now dormant field.

9. ENJOYING THE SCENERY

(September 1991)

WHAT SPECTACULAR WEATHER we observed this last month in Wyoming, Idaho and Montana during itineration. We enjoyed attractive variety every day, from high-mountain plateaus to low-land farming:

Awesome mountains often in view every day;

Magnificent stands of stately pine trees along the way;

Sparkling streams in unknown places catch our gaze;

Ducks gliding on hidden valley waterways;

Fish jumping in gorgeous rivers, a rare sight;

Clean air, fine food, with brilliant sunshine!

We were reminded of what God said in Genesis Chapter One when he created the world: "It is good." Indeed, creation beams with His goodness. Every rock, every tree, even every mountain has its own unique characteristics.

Similarly, in another spectacular way, the gracious people we met at every service made our itineration enjoyable and satisfying. Amid all the deadlines and dozens of services, fellowship with old acquaintances and the starting of new friendships fulfilled our days. Surely, "people" were why we itinerated.

People need Jesus;

People need the Word of God.

People need spiritual help, not tiny rhymes.

Jesus remains our only hope in troublesome times.

10. SNOW FLAKES AT DOLING PARK

(February 5, 2010)

QUARTER-SIZE SNOWFLAKES floated earthward with no sign of a chilling winter wind. I interrupted my walk on the indoor track of the Doling Fitness Center and paused by a window to look out and enjoy God's frigid beauty cast over a dormant world.

Leafless trees stood like broken statues and prickly bushes crouched over the once-green grass. A light glaze of sparkled silver covered the panorama before me.

This peaceful scenario reminded me of playing "Fox and Geese" as a youngster, even lying in the snow and moving my arms to create a pattern of angel wings while with wide-open mouth, I swallowed falling snow flakes.

My wife Mary and I thought a gigantic pillow had been torn open overhead. Its contents of feathery fluff upended over us, caused a powdered-sugar-like residue to blanket the bare ground. Those large geometric droplets descended slowly like the introduction to "I Know That My Redeemer Lives," from Handel's *Messiah*.

Each hexagon hung suspended by an invisible thread producing a delay during the downward fall inviting our personal inspection of each heavenly design of lingering wafers.

Seconds ceased, with time frozen in eternity; the splendor of the moment couched in immortality. Delicate bits of moisture loitered lazily with small spaces between each majestic flake.

Different intervals of spacing in the delayed motion of each ornately-shaped mass gave the effect of a Bach organ prelude performed in Westminster Abbey.

The Doling event was not a major winter storm, nor a blizzard, nor a late-season squall. To me, this pastoral setting paralleled the snow scene in the 1954 movie *White Christmas*.

The shimmering cascade of these architectural marvels soon began to dwindle in size and clarity, resulting in the dulling of this impressive experience.

The temperature rose to 34^0F. and large beads of moisture splashed noisily on the windows signaling the beginning of a light drizzle. The gradual transition encouraged the fields of nearby grass to exhibit a hint of hoped-for summer greenness.

The kaleidoscopic view of winter wonder changed every few minutes. I knew these flurries had occurred between two howling storms, one traveling nearby, the other one soon to pass overhead.

What had caused this amazing pocket of secluded calmness? Was the harshness of brutally cold weather returning to delay any thought of the nearness of spring? Was the brutality of an arctic cold-air mass being defused by storms ascending from the warm Gulf waters? I only knew God's artistry of filigreed snow symmetry reigned supreme this morning.

Two days earlier, the 100-plus resident Canada geese pecked through the snow at the base of trees in the surrounding park. They laboriously managed a snack in small open grassy areas.

Today, amid the melting snow and rising temperatures, those magnificent guests were free again to roam the grassland carpets for their meals, compliments of the Creator.

For me, this fifth snow storm of the season provided an impressive visual blessing from the Lord for both the geese and for Mary and me.

11. THE SPIRIT OF STURGIS

(October 13, 2014)

VAROOM CHUGGA-LUGGA-Brugga! The start-up procedure and sound of the three shiny, Harley Davidson
"Hogs" belonging to my neighbor's retired military sons, rever-
berated violently in the open, double-car garage.

At last the truth surfaced. The spirit of Sturgis rose up
yet another time for this trio to praise the Lord to those they
daily encounter. They had started their engines simultaneously
like a kindly resurgence, a gentle witness of the might and
power of the cool, calculated, and measured spirit of Teddy
Roosevelt's Roughriders.

The roar caused tools on the walls to chatter. Some fell
off their hooks, disturbing the quietness of nearby homes. The

confusion alarmed the seven turkeys grazing in their backyard clustered near their bird feeders.

It frightened the five geese flying low on a northerly course in formation and preparing to land on the Village pond just over the trees. But now, flustered in trying to maintain order in their V-formation—neighbor's front doors flew open. Each couple wondering if a large thunder cloud might be dropping buckets-full of quarter-sized hail in their front yards.

Or if a triple-car fender bender had piled up in someone's front yard. Or if a thirty-foot deep sink hole had swallowed a sizeable portion of our side street. Perhaps the kids at the local high school, only six blocks away, had conducted an early Halloween science experiment involving the elements of gun powder for the next Friday night football game and band half-time show.

However, one of those gorgeous Harley "Hogs" motored down our avenue humming like a purring tom cat after eating a succulent fish dinner. Although a few throttled backfires erupted to emphasize an emotional good bye, which might cause one to think the rider may be a modern day Gene Autry or Roy Rodgers, waving adios with his weather-worn wide-brimmed Stetson.

Instead, the rider secured the strap on his football-like helmet, fully equipped with sun visor and built-in telephone system. Who knows? He might soon be rolling along shortly toward Sturgis, South Dakota, and the annual motorcycle rally attended by hundreds of other enthusiasts.

Well, probably he might be taking only a short ride to the neighborhood gas station. But he could be returning in these early morning hours to his Kansas home with his two brothers. Each brother owns a similarly fully-equipped and reliable, over-the-road, two-wheeler Harley.

Some neighbors not seeing a disaster, surely thought heaven popped open. They expected to see Jesus.

A tear-drop of remembrance spotted my neighbor's cheek at their departure. An emotional sigh brought forth memories of his three riders' childhood escapades.

Once again he beamed with fatherly pride. "Good bye, my sons. Your mother and I look forward to seeing you next time. You know where we live. Come back soon. We love you."

IV. PIECEMEAL POETIC PRATTLE

1. A DRIVING MANUAL FOR METRO MANILA

(1984)

DRIVING IN METRO MANILA tests a person's reflexes, resolve, and courage. Within the first two months of our arrival at the Far East Advanced School of Theology (FEAST) in August 1982, I recorded my reactions to Asian traffic.

This type of driving became more difficult than cruising on the open roads of North and South Dakota where a person might meet only a few vehicles within a one-hundred-mile stretch of relative straight highway.

For every ten vehicles moving in city traffic, there might be one truck, two trikes, two *jeepneys*, one car, two buses and two motor bikes. The motorized growth of the City gave the appearance of an energetic and indefatigable beehive in which we soon might have no space to drive.

The Philippines' *jeepney* was developed from the U.S. Army WW II jeep and lengthened to accommodate two long bench seats placed parallel inside the covered, passenger area. The outer sides of the vehicle are decorated with pictorial artwork; small statues of horses are mounted on the hood representing the *calesa* (horse-drawn cart and taxi of pre-WW II days).

"His front bumper," explained Ken, "stands ahead of ours.

He has the right-of-way, don't give him any glowers.

The road space ahead," Ken instructed, "now empty and open,

He may move there with nothing hopefully broken."

My driving lessons continued amid great concentration,

Absorbing his profound declarations.

My wifie dear advised though

With this proverb: "Go, with the flow."

Observant Brother H. responded exactly:

"Metro Manila traveling I leave to a taxi.

It's not worth the trouble or a smashed mess.

Iligan City traffic gives me no stress."

Said wise old Les: "You will know the inner person.

A person's deep feelings sometimes worsen

By the way he drives in Metro Manila.

At the wheel, when acting like a gorilla."

I soloed in rivulets of perspiration the third day.

    I drive most days a mini-Indianapolis 500 Speedway,

Lost only once in Quezon City, but not far,

    Sailing in our dependable Speed-the-Light (STL) car.

Gear up, gear down, we repeatedly touch

    One's left toe on the tip of the clutch.

Keep your right hand on the gear shift as you ride,

    Bumper to bumper, eyes ahead and to each side.

Driving in the City we measure in minutes,

    Sometimes hours, these are the limits.

Blossoms a symphony of sounds, daily the norm,

    Amid the blowing of loud bugles beside my horn.

Innumerable buses changing their lane,

    Like fleeing rabbits, they become a bane.

Hundreds of *jeepneys* stop in the middle

    Of lanes, for passengers which can be a riddle.

Large numbers of trucks, many with a delivery bed,

    Increasing numbers of petite cars forging ahead,

The freighters stagger under heavy precarious loads,

    Clogging the already congested old roads.

Most accidents cause buses and *jeepneys* a tow,

    Daily downed freight trucks snarl the traffic flow.

Busy pedestrians must learn the road pace,

    But all, even a carabao, has a right to his space.

Drift right or fade left to keep alive.

    In heavy traffic, 2 lanes become 3, 3 grow to 5.

Expect to ignore a white lane marker.

    Learn to maneuver through six lanes, or park her.

Watch the road conditions; broken glass takes its toll.

    Pools of rain water may cover an open man-hole.

Bad weather causes big holes in the road and bumps.

    Each second requires attention to people and cars.

Blinking lights and a too-daa-toot can mean:

"I want to come through."

Don't forget to check out your night driving, too.

Beside more hazards, most vehicle lights are turned

off at a stop light.

While vehicle horns play Strauss or a

Sousa melody bright.

While the air-con remains on and you're stopped

at a corner,

Advance the gas, then you won't be a mourner.

Carry an umbrella when you step out on the street.

Cover the steering wheel with a towel in the heat.

Don't take anything for sure.

Lock your car, you leave a thief not a lure.

Left-turn lights may denote

"I want through" or "I'm going slow," so detour.

Charles T. Clauser

Left-hand turns are made from lanes that are narrow

On a red light with green arrow.

Or stay on the right lane shoulder to confirm.

Then scoot when the Patrolman signals the turn.

Happy Driving! It won't take long

to recognize enroute

A beep, taata-taata daa, or a blaaauw

from a toot-toot!

2. MIKE'S MOLDY BOOTS

(January 23, 2012)

HIS BOOTS GREW MOLD along each sole,
Foretold a problem big and old.

Young Mike looked down and found a hole,

His toe came through the front-end fold.

He thought he bought those boots '08,

The cost he knew came high for him.

Too tight, too small, too stiff, bad mate,

His coach said, "do not come to the gym."

He felt he better clean his boots,

Before his dad looked down and said:

"Young man, it looks like growing roots.

Today make clean and repair with Fred."

Friend Fred knew how to sew and shine,

Each boot or shoe brought in to his shop.

Young rascal Mike paid six bucks nine,

Before his dad might see more rot.

Each day he walked to school in dread,

Of Head Man Ted who checked each boy.

'Twas fun to scuff each toe instead,

And use each boot or shoe like a toy.

Now Ted had said to all the class,

Be good to both your shoes and feet.

Please note, your foot gear are not brass,

But made for feet to stand the heat.

First grade was tough for Mike and his boots,

    He knew the rules both home and at

      school.

He felt alone, with adults in cahoots,

    The tyke said, "I will not be a fool."

He learned to clean and shine the leather,

    Until he saw in his boots a picture.

Friend Fred said, "Come, let's work together,

    I'll teach you my trade, we'll start with

      Scripture.

"I lace all footwear tight with prayer,

    And cut and glue and sew with care.

Now Mike, I offer you a dare,

    Come work and learn to match each pair."

Young Mike stood tall and straight at age ten,

    He made fine boots and belts and shoes.

"Goodbye green mold and holes that offend."

    Mike's faith expressed Friend Fred's Good News.

3. BUTCH AND THE MISSING COOKIES

(January 16, 2012)

A LVA LOOKED AROUND out doors for Ken,
Games he often played with Joe and Ben.

"Why did you kids go hide in the woods and pretend?

I made chocolate cookies, come to our den."

Ben came first and begged, "I'll eat ten."

Joe informed their gang, "Amen, amen."

Ken just laughed, agreed and winked at a friend,

Sister, please bring more, we you commend."

Carol, my mom, set food upon the table,

    Old-dog Butch did howl for sweets from Mabel.

Alva brought more rolls desired by the youth.

    Butch they caught at the scene surprised in his goof.

Daniel found but two remains quite late.

    Ken's surprise continued in fake-like hate.

Butch had gulped just eight before all ate.

    God's surprises continued at Butch's ill fate.

Ellen next door came in for coffee and cake.

    Alva told her of the dog's last dreadful state.

He was banned from the house in terrible shame.

    Bad-dog Butch now lives at the end of a chain.

4. BEWARE: NO ESCAPE FROM SIN

(March 27, 2015)

So MANY THINGS made fake,

It makes us want to hate.

They think we'll take the bait,

A false, unhappy state.

We caught them stealing cake.

They tried to jump the gate.

Both fell and dropped a plate,

Their scheme for loot, not great.

To jail, they found their fate.

Then Jake and Kate called Nate.

"Please pay the rate, dear mate.

We know we can't escape!

Oh, how to correlate,

We must corroborate."

No dates awhile you wait.

The Chief will hold your freight.

They dreamed of life too late,

On winter ice to skate.

Hot sun, bare feet, no cape.

Now gone, their tête-à-tête!

5. CHECK OUT THAT BALD-HEADED PREACHER

(October 9, 2015)

OH MY, OH MY, can that man preach!
We watch most nights at half-past six.

His word-play cuts us to the quick.

He wrote a book with which to teach.

His flock of thousands love the mix.

They stand and shout accepting pricks.

Charles T. Clauser

Amazing how he moves his reach,

To gather sinners for God's fix.

They savor every building brick.

Some come maybe from a beach,

Arrived and ready for a pix.

Desiring first, 'what makes life tick!'

They learn all sin in life must bleach

And cease! For Jesus' love, it sticks,

Forever burns His flowing wick.

Forever gone the hungry leech.

God shows the future without ticks.

Our Jesus gives a daily kick.

That bald-headed man will shout each night,

"Keep on, keep on, the Lord makes right!"

Will you, too, follow God's invite?

6. TWO LOVELY LADIES

(January 17, 1998)

Two Lovely Ladies   Two Football Fans

    They really write   They never knew

        Listen Lucky Lassies   Listen Michi -- ganders

           I'm bragging big   I'm a marching man

              Dad Caring Chorister!   Dad Trombone Tooter!

Two Bashful Bells   Two hardy Hearts

   They cuddle kitties   Their golfing goofed

     Listen Dainty Darlings   Listen Playing Partners

    I'm a eating easy   I'm an eighty even

Dad Fussy Foot!	Dad Sixty-Six!
Two Cozy Coeds	Two Sleepy Sals
They growl grandly	They daily drop
Listen Bossy Babes	Listen Slumbering Suzies
I'm a tearful teddy	I'm a nodding now
Dad Hurting Heart!	Dad Nosey Napper
Two Daring Damsels	Two Spunky Speakers
They plenty print	They revised Robert's
Listen Proven Pals	Listen Dinner Dames
I'm a worry wart	I'm a counting corn
Dad Tommy Tiger!	Dad Laughing Loose
Two Smiling Sisters	Two Snappy Snickers
They frolic fishing	They needed news
Listen Outdoor Otters	Listen Network Neighbors
I'm a happy helper	I'm an itchy icon
Dad Grinning Grandpa	Dad Wordy Wit
Two Serious Singles	Two Penny Pinchers

They seldom sit	They value veggies
Listen Plucky People	Listen City Chums
I'm a praying pastor	I'm a perky papa
Dad Fancy Farmer!	Dad Pretty Proud

V. TEA TIME TIDBITS

1. SPRING

(These four sets of poems were written April/May 2011)

SPRING SYMPHONY (Rhythms of Life)

Look closely,

new tulips

and daffodils,

beautiful crocus.

Smell the earthy fragrance.

Feel rhythms of budding life.

Enjoy multiple sounds of life.

Grasp the smooth energy of nature.

Hear birds and bees in rhapsodic choirs.

SPRING SUDS (Clean, Scrub, Paint)

CLEAN YOUR ROOM and wash the car,

Rake the garden, plant corn seed.

Mow the grass, build compost trash,

Scrub the cupboards, launder socks.

Sweep the workshop, clean off tar,

Spray for spiders, white my creed.

Paint the barn and sell old Nash,

Water plants, remove the rocks.

Scrub the tub, replace soap bar,

Trim the bushes, do not bleed.

Pull out weeds, wear gloves no rash,

Bossy cow approves and talks.

SPRING SWEETHEART (Two Good Friends)

ALLURING LADY proudly would,

Behind young Matthew's feet spread wide.

Her hair washed clean felt soft like silk,

His locks when washed shone curled like waves.

The two good friends each understood,

Each other's habits need abide.

For food they chose abundant milk,

Which showed their wishes all their days.

For two small kitties very good,

They purred beside the dog inside.

His bowl of food they thought to bilk,

The three in play enjoyed our praise.

SPRING HAIKU (The Goslings)

THE NASTY CLOUDS splashed,

Sending geese up the ravine.

Can goslings survive?

Loud the angry quacks,

Escape the flood my darlings!

Climb, climb, we shall help.

Sit on this large rock,

Safe beneath the small o'er hang.

Learn the water strength.

Charles T. Clauser

SPRING BASEBALL (Shorty and Daisy)

COME TO MY GAME we begin mid-day.

Shorty and Daisy will play with us.

Classes are cancelled for Easter time.

Members are short, but we all can hit.

Out on the field we run fast to play.

Sometimes our games are delayed by Russ.

Coaching became his main love his line.

Players showed gratitude for his wit.

Shorty and Daisy retrieved kid's way.

Proud cocker spaniels chased balls no fuss.

Each will arrive to bark loudly "Mine!"

Challenging barks with no baseball mitt.

SPRING HOME GOING (Grandma Stella)

GRANDMA STELLA AGE ninety-six last,

Came from Kansas, taught Sunday School lore.

Beloved mother, great, great, grand with class,

Children four, from those eight, then five more.

I met Stella one Wednesday in church,

Sitting back near the rear a short pew.

I ask why she was left in the lurch,

With no people near I saw my cue.

May I sit with you here as we sing?

"You may join me with hymn book tonight."

With a twinkle in eyes low she beamed,

Lord, a beautiful face she brings light.

SPRING CLOUDS (Bad Storms)

TODAY I PRAY THE storms will go away,

We sing, we shout, we clap our hands, we praise.

Please join us praying daily safety, okay?

Do make your schedule filled with prayer all days.

The Lord will answer you and me each time,

We come to Him with a humble heart that's pure.

Depart bad storms of useless beer and wine,

Resolve, rededicate to God for cure.

Find peace and love and grace and joy within,

The day came bright our prayer was right for all.

Our group sat down to win with two a twin,

We saw and felt those storm clouds stall and fall.

You clouds of sin, of hate and lies be gone,

Forever take God's Son and leave the wrong

2. SUMMER

SUMMER SCORCHER (Storms and Corn)

S WEAT
 OOZES

from my arms,

drips off my brow.

The sun turns skin brown,

Electrical storms surge.

Aurora borealis

sparkles wide and bright on clear nights.

Listen to the growing corn crackle,

pigs root, chickens scratch, cows browse

  contented.

Charles T. Clauser

SUMMER SAILING (Racing with the Wind)

GENTLE WIND ALONG the shoreline,

Cruising crossways shallow ridges.

Setting course up wind out harbor,

Raising mainsail high and lofty.

Puffy clouds ahead may pour nine,

Come-about downwind by bridges.

Shortened route we turned back starboard,

Safely home-bound waters frothy.

Racing with the wind behind us,

Neck and neck with friends no hitches.

Dock in sight because comes the down pour,

Batten hatches, waves all choppy.

Lower sails, secure the dock lines,

Run for cover, rain fills ditches.

Short the squall line, open car door,

"Son, let's eat, please pass the coffee."

SUMMER SHOPPING (Henry's Five and Dime)

WE SHOPPED AT HENRY'S Five and Dime,

His store displays all candy made.

Up front he serves all kinds of shakes,

He even cooks thick burgers lean.

Behind the winter stove you'll find,

The pants and shirts still nicely laid.

A blouse, a skirt for outside dates,

A dress, new shoes the growing teen.

Debate each day the oldsters shine,

Old Henry eyes all sales be paid.

Young women come to sell their cakes,

An onion, carrot, turnip, bean.

SUMMER HAIKU (Rain and Hail)

STORM CLOUDS BUILD out West,

Rain and hail pelt homes and trees.

Take cover wee ones.

All day cold rain fell,

Dark skies exploded white light.

Thunder hurt my ears.

Will tomorrow shine?

Clear, bright, warm, a perfect day?

The hot sun will know.

SUMMER FRIEND (Mary Jane)

DOWN BY THE CREEK we saw Mary Jane,
Sprawled on a rock soaking sunny rays.

Mother and brothers and sisters lain,

Nearby on grass unconcerned nor fazed.

There was a hole by the tree main root,

Water rose high one day causing fear.

Owl in tree sounded alarm with hoot,

None of the family woke to hear.

High in the den sat Lil' Mary Jane,

Family members all drowned so quick.

290

She only lived to tell how came rain,

Dear little skunk became tame with Dick.

SUMMER VACATION (The Lakeside Resort)

AT THE LAKESIDE RESORT we can fish,
For small trout, tasty crappie and bass.

Can't we daily go swimming I wish,

Mom said yes, Dad said no, guess I'll pass.

Let's go hiking instead after lunch,

Yonder hill will be high says my hunch.

We need boots a nice snack we can munch,

We should find all the guys a big bunch.

See that cloud, it will rain half past one.

I don't like it, not fair for our fun.

Shall we bowl one more line or do none?

Weather won, came the sun, we shall run.

SUMMER HEAT (Young Bill Died)

I HEARD YOUNG BILL last summer died of heat.
He didn't drink the water grandma pumped.

Charles T. Clauser

His gang was playing up and down the street.

Young Bill ran fast but hit a block, got bumped.

The game you might surmise they called tag ball.

Young Bill they named El Capitan the Great.

Both teams were fierce when playing on the mall.

One team wore blue the other red for mates.

The score came close that day as each made goals.

Each clock was set to ring at half past three.

Some moms and dads began to stand like poles.

Such action caused adults to shout with glee.

But look! An Accident! A Pile-up play.

The bottom man Bill won't see another day.

3. FALL

FALL FEATURES (Garden Produce)

SQUASH,

PUMPKINS,

prunes, apples

and potatoes

filling baskets, jars,

barrels amid canning

activities on the farm.

In the city, farm markets make

space for home-grown garden produce and

specialty gift items to line the home.

FALL FLIGHT (Thousands Flying High)

GEESE AND DUCKS LIKE planes abound,

Countless squadrons fill the sky.

Change of season signals flight,

Food and rest stops marked en route.

Groups of wrens no longer found,

Birds by thousands flying high.

Robins, grackles leave our site,

Humming birds don't gad about.

Dreary, stark and quiet round,

Sunless days and lonesome guy.

Bare the fields the land of might,

Birds will come again no doubt.

FALL FRENZY (The School Bus)

THE SCHOOL BUS RIGHT on time, I'm late,

Alarm bell dinged I slept on through.

'Twas late last night a movie long,

It scared me all night long in the dark.

She came and tuck me in, Mom Kate.

"Oh, please don't leave me here I'll stew.

With shades all drawn I need a song."

"Okay, we'll sing together Mark."

The school bus will no longer wait,

Your teacher bright will see through you.

Confess, come clean, you did quite wrong,

Get up and make a brand new start.

FALL HAIKU (School Contests)

FOOTBALL, SOCCER games,

Contests, after-school practice.

Drill every day.

Pete fade right downfield,

Sally, block that kick through Buzz.

Think ahead defense.

Winners reliable,

Losers fade away each day.

The Lord provides help.

FALL HARVEST (The Pumpkin Patch)

BIG THEY DID GROW in the patch for Dad,

Yellow the color I told my Sis.

Please Mommy bake a nice pie for us,

Serve it with ice cream and cookies, too.

Fellows from town came out young and bad,

Did they want pumpkins to give their Miss?

"No," each said looking instead to Gus.

Why was their purpose to come and stew?

Strawberries, raspberries, made them glad,

Stealing rip produce they thought it bliss.

Bringing the shotgun my Dad made a fuss,

Mom brought hot pie as if called on cue.

Sis blew them kisses, but Dad so mad,

Charged them all double then shooed with fist.

Hanging their heads they left learning trust.

Pumpkins galore now what might you do?

FALL FABLE (Sir Sam and the Hound)

BETWEEN PILES OF DRY leaves sat Sir Sam,

A black squirrel of fame all around.

Full of play teasing birds a big ham,

"I will catch you today," barked the Hound.

"You're too slow," spoke up Sam as he fled,

Climbing Tootsie the tree, up he ran.

"Best you pardon me I am not dead,"

Chortled Hound with his coat of bright tan.

With the wind Tootsie shook Sir Sam down,

In-charge Hound bayed loud: "give me your hand!

I don't bite only growl this side town.

Let's be friends and impress our house clan."

"Our yard play comes each day we don't clown,"

Said Sir Sam swishing tail cocking head.

"A long truce for a mid-day sleep sound,

Will help friends keep the peace," replied Hound.

FALL GATHERING (Young Mike)

THE MONTH OF CLASSES started right for Mike.

First grade was new for classmates black and brown.

The group included friends both red and white.

Their teacher Sweet Miss Nancy lived in town.

Each student gave their parent's name that day.

Young Mike was bold and said, "My name spells gold."

The class then laughed, but Sweet Miss Nanc' did stay.

She spoke her name -- Miss Silver, once was sold.

Now quiet, eager ears to learn her Braille,

Knelt down beside her desk with eyes quite wide.

"To help each other live together hale.

Remember Mike, in God we must abide."

Born blind and red she spoke as one who knew,

Born black and cross-eyed, Mike then learned what's true.

4. WINTER

WINTER WOES (Quilted Cocoon)

COLD DAYTIME,

bitter night

temperature,

blankets piled high,

quilt cocoons encasing

beds placed far from heat vents or

fireplaces burning low each night.

Dead – the fire, the heat, the light, the warmth.

Low the thermostat, sleepy heads now wake.

WINTER WONDERS (The Ski Slope)

CRISP AIR BRIGHT SUN glares on snow,

Warm gloves big coat glasses tint.

Hot tea, coffee, milk in cups,

Keep the fireplace stoked all night.

Wide the ski slope people flow,

Downhill courses marked in print.

Fees and clothes do cost big bucks,

Teachers help you learn what's right.

Supper time and wind will blow,

Birthday boy loud speaks a hint.

Mommy dog gave birth to pups,

Christmas trees snow-covered bright.

WINTER WARMTH (A Bear Den)

A BEAR STAYS WARM when snuggled up,
In winter cold by digging down.

A den well-hidden you won't see,

In snow or brush or cave can hide.

The black, the brown, the grizzly, we duck,

Because we find them wide around.

In western parts they roam most free,

And scare each on a horse-back ride.

Before each spring when chicks each cluck,

Small cubs emerge from winter's sound.

Mom bear might dream of honey bee,

And goes outside the twins to guide.

WINTER HAIKU (Birthday Snow)

YOUNG LADY LOOKED out,

Her bedroom window at dawn.

A blanket of snow.

The cardinal sang,

A blue jay screeched loud for food.

Two rabbits left tracks.

"Get dressed my fair girl,

A hot breakfast coming up.

Happy Birthday, Lass!"

Charles T. Clauser
WINTER TRAVEL (Power Lines Swayed)

SNOW BLEW ACROSS ICY roads that day,

Power lines swayed back and forth -- scary.

Travel by van we were caused to pray:

"God we need You on this bare prairie."

Driving was slow with both wheels on rock,

Right side we found hard with ground, less ice.

Drivers abandoned this road to talk,

Coffee and rolls while they played with dice.

We went on trusting the Lord each hour,

Rugby our ministry goal that night.

God's helping hand came to show power.

Safely we traveled through snow no fright.

WINTER CHILI (Mom's Basement Food Supply)

IN OUR BASEMENT MOM placed many cans

Of cooked chili with fruit all down stairs.

Growing up we helped Mom prepare pans

Of sweet corn, little peas, cucs and pears.

Then came processing plants near each town,

Fifteen miles away tanks were turned hot.

But next year our hometown processed fruit,

They prepared most delicious stock.

I like chili with cornbread served brown,

For our lunch even supper or snack.

No more custom home-canning in town,

"Will you join me in eating, Sir Jack?"

WINTER CONCERTS (A Symphonic Season)

THE TRUMPETS SCREAMED, the trombones blared parts.

Two oboes whined, four horns sublime in time.

Bassoons played low as flutes ran skyward darts.

The strings were mellow, no one left behind.

An overture by Wagner warmed the crowd.

A Mozart symphony pleased those who heard,

Attendees far and near said, "Why so loud?"

Rachmaninoff subdued the claim -- absurd.

Charles T. Clauser

Concerto style made him be great and liked.

Tchaikovsky tops the list of works not pale.

And Verdi wrote his scenes, but never miked.

Puccini's Tosca tells a gruesome tale.

Our seats we found in Mezzanine Row L.

Sit down, relax, enjoy. They rang the bell.

VI. FRIENDSHIP FOCUSED FABLES

1. KICKER KEITH'S FOOTBALL DREAM

(October 15, 2010)

W AKE UP, KEITH! The Packer game will begin in five minutes."

"Okay, dear."

Ermalene, reclined nearby in her favorite lounge chair and sipped a cup of hot Echinacea tea topped with a spoonful of honey. She looked at Keith in bewilderment.

Keith sat in his recliner attempting to read the Sunday paper, patiently waiting for the final Packer game of the season to begin. The afternoon sun shone through large windows warming the living room.

Crimson leaves, spiraling down like toy tops beneath the front yard maple trees had begun their autumn pageantry.

The radiant heat of the day caused Keith's eyes to lose focus as he relaxed with feet propped up, resting comfortably and becoming nearly supine in his overstuffed chair.

Drowsiness gave way to the labored breathing of a noisy nose-whistle symphony accompanied by the fluttering of leaves, rhythmically and almost silently tapping the windows behind Keith's back.

Parts of his paper fell to the floor. His head slumped gently backward resting on the soft neck cushion allowing the sports section to slowly settle across his lap.

"Shall I wake him?" she pondered, "or shall I let him sleep?

The game will commence in fifteen minutes. I know he really wants to see it. I'll wait a few minutes to awaken him. That way, he will be able to enjoy the contest and not feel tired."

Sipping her tea, she surmised: "He worked hard this week. I'll let him sleep a bit. He needs the rest. In the meantime, I shall glance through the feature and headline news sections."

Keith meanwhile fell into a deeper sleep accompanied with unusually loud and intermittent snoring. Being completely relaxed, he began to dream —a dream of make-believe, involving his special football artifacts and souvenirs, who had become special friends.

"Come a runnin' friends, to the football game – Green Bay Packers, hurrah! The league championship teams face off today," announced the Little Packer Salt Shaker, skipping along the table rim.

"Game time, fifteen past two—okay. Alert our cheering squad. We expect a win," squealed the Small Packer Pepper Holder, romping with his twin.

"Hey, hey! Keith wearing his cheese hat—surely means a Packer win in this fierce scrap," hiccupped Ermalene's Bright-Green Packer Cup, responding to the cheering challenge.

"I like Keith's Woolly-Green Packer Socks," added the Shiny Ornamental Packer Spoon hanging on the game room wall. "Just right for shuffling his feet in that cozy reclining chair."

"Take me quick to this ballgame foe, every inch of that turf I know," Yelled the Glassed-In Pigskin Trophy. "I'll show my grandson how to fly, in sun or rain whether hot or cold weather, we'll sail through the sky. Then each bullet pass completed shall be remembered like fine poetry."

"Don't forget me! Take me, please, please," pleaded the Extra-Long Silk Packer Scarf. "A breath of fresh air will stop my wheeze. Get me out of this stuffy plastic bag; I need a fresh breeze."

As the game began, the Packers won the coin toss. Kick off received! Then first and ten on the 22-yard line. The well-matched teams fought furiously.

Meanwhile, dancing around the dining room table, Pepper Holder did cheer, "Fake a pass, but drive through the center line of nine."

One player, however, from each side soon became benched with excessive knee pain. Minutes later, the scoreboard reported: second quarter, only two minutes remain.

"Pigskin, call out your best Packer passing play," urged Extra-Long Silk Scarf. "You'll save the day."

"No, no," opposed Little Packer Salt Shaker, beginning to lose her self-control. "Signal for the half-back to kick a field goal."

"Watch out, charge right! Hide the ball," bellowed Ermalene's Bright-Green Packer Cup.

As the conflict continued, Shiny Ornamental Packer Spoon cried out, "Yippee," chattering encouraging comments as he bounced along the wall. "Look at that Packer quarterback move downfield. He moves faster than a Gazelle; he surely could out-run a truck.

"Yeah, touch down! Strike up the Packer band! Six and 0. But will they make that slick kick?"

Woolly-Green Socks covered his eyes, too scared to look at the kicker man. "Yes, excellent," he declared, peeking at last. "This seven shall stick." Once again the tension increased, emotions nearly exploded. The next check on time: fourth quarter; score – ten/ten.

Shiny Ornamental Spoon jitterbugged over to Little Salt Shaker exclaiming, "We dare not, we must not fall behind. Tell Pigskin to set up that special end-run play for the Packer team. He listens to you, even when pretending to be supreme."

Oops! Trouble! "Packers offside; a penalty, a ten-yard fine," called out the Ref straddling the twenty-yard line.

"Woolly-Green Socks help Keith propel this next play past the guards, through the tackle and left line," snorted Pepper Holder.

Ermalene's Bright-Green Cup brimmed with coffee parked by a roll. Extra-Long Silk Scarf flipped around excitedly like a snake whip. Shiny Ornamental Spoon tap danced in anticipation of a field goal.

The Little Packer Shaker burped salt enthusiastically nearly throwing a fit. Pepper Holder sneezed game plays to Pigskin previously seldom used.

Glassed-In Pigskin Trophy panted breathlessly beginning his spiel: "Five and goal, fifty-one seconds to game – we shall not lose." Everyone wondered, will this rivalry end in a tie? But wait! "What's this on the field?" shouted Glassed-In Pigskin Trophy. "I don't believe it! Too much time in the huddle."

"The refs assessed a fifteen-yard penalty against the Packers," shouted the Little Salt Shaker, falling on her side in disbelief. "By my Aunt Regret who won the Kentucky Derby, I'll salt that Ref's water bottle."

"Pigskin," the Little Salt Shaker continued after regaining her composure, "Round up Packer Spoon and Pepper Holder. Text Woolly-Green Socks and Ermalene's Packer Cup.

Tell Extra-Long Silk Scarf to snap to. Sound the alarm, send the word. We want field goal Kicker Keith"

Everyone was talking at the same time. Even Packer Pennant, Packer Sweater, and Packer Rain Jacket joined these unusual cheer leaders. No one would settle for less than a definitive win.

"Altogether gang," the Little Salt Shaker declared. "Pigskin, lead us in a Packer cheer!"

They all shouted: "We want Kicker Keith! We want Kicker Keith!" The chanting grew louder and more intense.

"Give us a 'K'" --------- "K"

"Make it a big 'E'" ----- "E"

"Remember the 'I'" -----"I"

"Grow a mighty 'T'" ---"T"

"Shout a Packer 'H'" ---"H"

"What does it spell?" ----"K-E-I-T-H." This remarkable cheering squad kept chanting: "We want Kicker Keith!"

To their jubilation, the Packer coach ran to the edge of the field and signaled a time out, the last one allowed for his team. He sent in Kicker Keith amid shouts of approval and thunderous applause.

Then, the contrast of complete silence – no one in the stadium breathed. No crows squawked. Even the Goodyear Balloon floating overhead eavesdropping held steady.

The center snapped the ball directly to the halfback who placed it expertly on angle for Kicker Keith. Although only seconds were needed for the kick, it seemed like eternity passed waiting for its completion.

Up—up—higher—traveling farther—spinning toward the goal posts. Every eye anxiously watched its flight. The kick took place on the twenty-five yard line, an enormous distance to successfully send Pigskin's grandson.

Darkness was near; the high-intensity stadium lights were turned on. A fifteen-mile an hour crosswind had caused many persons to button their jackets and roll up their collars. It looked like, by those persons sitting at the fifty-yard line, the ball might hit the left pole, possibly fall a bit short.

But no! The kick was successful! And throughout the stadium rolled the Packer victory chant again and again: "Kicker Keith, our hero!"

"Keith . . . Keith," Ermalene spoke softly, but firmly, touching his forearm gently with a slight twist of her fingers. "Wake up, Dear. The football game is almost over. I also fell asleep reading the paper.

"Butch, our neighbor's dog, barked as their children took him for a walk past our front yard. That raucous sound awakened me. Turn up the TV volume. We'll be able to watch the last few plays of the game and know the final score."

And that, ladies and gentlemen, recounts the fabulous incident of how Packer Man Keith came late into this extraordinary Green Bay encounter and kicked a field goal for the famous Packers.

He broke the tie that year with nine seconds remaining in a most memorable league championship struggle. Final score: 13 to 10 in favor of the triumphant Green Bay Packers.

2. TWO WHEELBARROW BUDDIES

(March 8, 2014)

W HAT KIND OF ACTIVITIES might those two pieces of equipment share if given personalities?" I wondered.

While writing his memoirs, my brother-in-law described a photograph to me he found in a family album. The picture showed two persons, a four-year-old boy standing behind a child's wheelbarrow and an adult holding the handles of a regular-sized wheelbarrow.

Please visualize in your mind a spring morning in southwestern-central Michigan. Two inanimate objects, wheelbarrows, imbued with life; a dad and his four-year-old son working side by side on a commercial, row-crop farm. Blue birds sing in the trees, robins wander in the grass eating worms, even forage for bugs.

Papa Sam and his Little Jake – these two barnyard implements, toil for Auntie Blue and her young son, Smilin' Norm on her tulip farm. Days grow warm, the tulips stand tall, their colors shine rich and full.

At night, Dad Sam and Little Jocko sleep in the barn. It's their home. Both came to life when carved in its wood shop.

Good folks in the county see them labor each day. They know father and son stay busy this way.

Miz' Auntie Blue sometimes rewards them with raspberry pie. Once, she baked a chocolate cake and chimed "My, oh my. Before you put it away, you both must sit down and pray."

"Let me help today," Little Jake whimpered. A tear drop dribbled down his cheek. "You'll see, Papa dear, my rig will hold a full load, never fear."

"Okay, Lil' One. Fill up over by the barn, then bring your shovel and scoop. We shall till each row with young master, Smilin' Norm."

Moments later, Little Jake squealed, "Papa dear, I want to play in the dirt. It feels so soft under my wheel. Please, Papa, only a while?"

"No, Lil' One. Out here, we work steadily row by row over all the ground. However, on Sunday we shall rest. Then we can play. But first, we must worship the Lord on each Holy Day."

"Papa . . . please?"

"Come, son. A drink of water, a short rest, and a mid-morning snack under the trees will refresh us. Care for a cookie? See, Auntie Blue sent us hot raisin bread, too."

Later, with their jobs resumed, Little Jake spoke his mind, "Papa, I meant no harm."

"I know, Buddy Boy. For now, we'll help weed around the bulbs and green stems."

The two buddies also picked tulips and prepared their transport to market. On late summer days, they cleared the six acres in preparation for next year's crop, stopped only by the change of seasons and the coming fall rains. One season became two, then three, and quickly another. Suddenly, twenty years had passed.

Little Jake now became Papa Jake, and his little one received the name of Two Bits. Papa Sam retired that year when his large wooden bucket rotted through leaving three ragged holes.

A short time later, Papa Jake reminisced on Grandpa Sam's dying day out in the barn. "Pops, do you think the Lord will have use for us in heaven?"

"Certainly, Jocko. We could help the Holy Spirit encourage people by taking them a tulip, like we fulfilled our responsibilities down here all these years."

"Grandpa," Two Bits asked in her squeaky voice, "Do you think Jesus could use a small girl like me, up there with all the other tiny wheelbarrows?"

"Of course," Grandpa Sam beamed. "Next time you talk to Him and pray—ask Him!"

3. WHAT'S IN MY POCKET?

(Written 2014)

IF YOU CAN GUESS what I have in my pocket, you can have it." Jacie tantalized her ten-year old twin-brother Jed, as they tumbled out of the hay loft at the family farm in Billings, Missouri."

"Aw, you don't have nothin' in yer jean's pocket I'd want."

"I'll give you another clue, Smarty. It's not an arrow head."

"Wait . . . alfalfa dust . . . I cain't breathe. Gotta wash my face. Eyes burn."

"Me, too. Let's douse our eyes at the cattle trough."

"Ooh, the dust went through my clothes and shoes."

"Leave me some water. Just because you were born five minutes before me, don't make you chief rooster in the barnyard."

"I itch. But what fun to drop off the rope into loose hay."

"While you're washing, consider my second clue: you'll enjoy it."

"Never mind, if we don't get clean, Mom won't let us in the house for dinner."

Splash, splash!

"No good, I need a bath. Must be an inch of alfalfa dust all over me. I'm goin' for a swim in the cattle pond down by the creek. Mom will use Dad's leather strap on me, if I show for dinner after chores lookin' like a pile of hay. Wanna go skinny-dippin' with me?"

"Absolutely not! A girl doesn't do such a thing, and never with a naked boy."

"I thought I figured a slick way to get clean, even wash my clothes!"

"Excuse me! I'm going to clean up in the wood shed, then help Mom with dinner."

"You'll be sorry. My way sure beats bobbing in that soapy scum in the family tub."

. . . "You know, Jed, seventy years ago I was ready to disown you as my brother, because of your invitation to go bathing in a slimy pond. When we left the hay stack in Dad's barn, we looked like two broken bales of hay."

"I remember that day. For a moment, I thought you were some other person, not my sister."

"Every time I saw you throughout the next two days, my face turned red with anger. I didn't care to bathe in a pond laced with cow manure. That's why I withdrew my offer to give you something."

"Now, here we sit on Dad's front porch at the old homestead, celebrating our eightieth birthdays with our own children and grandkids."

"What a blessing. We must thank my daughter, Millie, and her twin girls for organizing this family event."

"I agree. I think Millie's my favorite niece."

"Jed, she's your only niece."

"That's why I think she's so super."

"By the way, I repented of my anger long ago. But I felt I might tease you today by placing a certain 70-year old something in my dress pocket. My third clue: you can use it regularly. Guess what it might be."

"You're spoofin' me. You've ask me the same question every ten years at our birthday parties. I never guess right when you quiz me. But this year, ah ha, I know the answer."

"Okay, Brother dear. Give me your best response."

"Do you remember the day, about two weeks after the alfalfa dust incident, you went to our farm neighbor's home, Shirley's birthday party?"

"Yes. We were best friends."

"On that day, I looked through every drawer and box in your room, searching for anything girls normally would not possess on a farm. I found your treasure in a small case under your blouses in the bottom dresser drawer—a small jack knife and scissor combination."

"Ooh, you Rascal! You lied to me at every one of our past birthday get-togethers."

"Yes, because I didn't want you to use Dad's leather strap on me for rummaging through your room. I knew I should wait for our 80th to tell you of my snooping. Then, I could confess to being a bad boy and beg your forgiveness with no penalty."

"Humph! You Scoundrel. I should have held your head under water at the cattle trough for suggesting nude bathing until you cried for mercy."

"I'm glad you didn't, Sis, because I think you're the best sister a guy could ever have. I love you."

"Alright, you Scalawag! Because it's our 80th, for both accounts, I forgive you, until I can find Dad's leather strap!

4. THAT KNOT WOULD NOT BUDGE

(Written January 11, 2014)

I TRIED AND TRIED. I pinched and pulled. I prayed and cleaned my glasses, but that knot would not budge. I thought, I shall pour water on it, but then I felt a douse of hand lotion might loosen that tight, tenacious, tough knot.

No success. No one in sight to help me. No tools, big or small to undo this idiotic, pernicious, unscheduled knot which stopped my activities of the day. Who will help me? Who might be coming this way? Someone will surely walk by any moment now. But I can't wait forever. This is decision time!

Oh, Jim! . . . Jim. Hey, buddy, come here please. I need your help. . . . Well, of all the . . . He walked right by me, as if he didn't see me. He didn't even say "hello." . . . Oh, here comes my friend, John, with his Bible. Just the man to assist me in my knotty situation.

"John, please come pray with me and help me undo this knot that will not budge. I'm desperate. What shall we do?" Oops, where did he go? He just vanished. That's not like John. He's a good man, a great counselor. That's not his character.

Lord Jesus, wherever you are this morning and in whatever job you're involved in on this cloudy day, please, please, put me on your schedule. This confounded knot will not budge.

It won't move up or fall down. I can't make it go backward or forward. It just sits there and seems to grow bigger every time I look at it.

Maybe, if I sing it a song it will come unraveled. Yes, yes. That will solve my problem. Holy Spirit, please help me.

"Oh knot that would not budge. Your time is done, all done. Tra-la-la, ra-hmm!"

Thank you Jesus! That twisted bed-sheet had me wrapped up, tied up, almost strangled, and hanging on the edge of my bed. I'll not take it to the laundromat again.

5. HOPE FOR TWO ABUSED SHOES

(August 22, 2012)

"SPUD, DID YOU CATCH a gander at those snazzy black shoes of Teach Kophew?"

"Yeah, sure did." Spud flipped his loose left shoe sole back in place as he looked over to Cricket. "I like the way those zippered inside panels mold to her ankles."

"Why didn't Mister Cobblerman do that for us?" Cricket, the right shoe of the pair of mismatched shoes, eyed one inside panel of her shoes then the other. "Humph, I feel he used all his left-over scraps to glue each of us together."

"Do you think," Spud spoke in his low voice, "he wanted us to plod along through life only as a protection for this youngster's feet?"

"One thing I know," Cricket replied standing on his semi-detached heel, "my sides ache, my back won't bend, my tongue gets yanked around my face, and my eyes now focus cross-eyed. This little kid with foot inserted, wraps me with knots each day."

Spud felt deflated. "If you think you have a problem, listen to mine. As keeper of the left shoe of our partnership, I wish to complain about our teenage owner. This morning in American history class, his left leg bounced up and down and sidewise whenever Teach Kophew mentioned either another date or Indian battle."

"I feel exhausted, too," Cricket sighed. "I wished this minor would settle down. I heard he begins middle school next year. When his stress level erupts, it causes my body to jitter-bug. My tattered sole may soon wear out, my broken heel fly away."

Spud tried to console his teammate. "Now Cricket, don't break a shoe string because of your pent-up anger at these emotional outbursts of Billy-boy's capers."

Cricket screeched in pain. He couldn't stop talking. "Do you know what happened before breakfast today? This undisciplined lad jammed his left foot into my innards made for his right foot. Then my real trouble started. He wore no socks. His foot smelled like the manure pile out behind the family barn. Phew! Putrid toes!"

"We may die of asphyxiation before old age cancels our usefulness," Spud gasped for air. "This lad likes to scuff my nose in the graveled parking lot at his school and the toe end of my sole now flaps like a bed sheet in the wind on a backyard clothes line."

"I know, he often forgets me on church day by making one fast swipe with a dirty cloth over my body—no clean face, no shine—just smears. It embarrasses me."

"Yeah, you would think he had enough sense to pour some Desenex powder into my arch to kill the itch. Disgusting! He needs basic training in a Marine boot camp.

"Buddy, I have an idea. Let's talk to those snazzy black shoes about our predicament. Perhaps they can persuade Teach Kophew to advise our young knight to wash his feet, medicate our inside seams, and shine our worn patches."

"You got it, Pard, tomorrow morning at class time." Spud, now hoarse, squeaked like a frog. "Let me do the talking. You might frighten her if she takes time to notice your special built-up, elevated shoe stitched together for Mister Fuss-Budget."

"Don't make fun of me," Cricket groaned as the stripling's foot in his inside parts squirmed side-to-side and heel-to-toe.

"A couple generous pats of boot grease spread around both your exterior and mine would ease your arthritis and cure my gout."

"I admit, I'm a sorrowful-looking collection of left-over, out-of-date, disheveled body parts. Nobody loves me and this adolescent in charge of us could care less about our appearance. Admit it Pard—we both need help beyond anything Teach Kophew or her black shoes might offer."

"You mean, someone like our maker, Mister Cobblerman, who might prescribe a remedy that attaches another glued patch on our sides, er . . . oh, I don't know what he might do. But I believe Mister Cobblerman could help us."

"Agreed. But how can we convince this juvenile to take us to Mister Cobblerman's shop?"

"Just move a nail up from your heel into your insole. It will cause this teeny bopper to scream for help. I need relief. Don't you? Aspirin won't do it."

"That action," Spud glowered, "would not show trust nor display honesty."

"Let's consider a better idea. Remember in church last Sunday, Pastor Kurltree spoke of Jesus the Savior? He then invited the youth to come forward at the end of the service and accept Jesus as Lord in their lives."

"For sure, eight young people went forward for salvation, but not our energetic schoolboy."

"True," Cricket thought for a moment about their problem. "Jesus, however, may be our answer. Pastor Kurltree said, 'Jesus not only forgives our sins, but will bless us, if we accept His kingship.' Pard, we both need a little red wagon – no, a big red wagon full of Jesus' blessings."

"Right on, Buddy, and I heard the pastor say that Jesus heals. If we tell Him of our difficult situation and ask for His help, I think He will somehow renew our patchwork of assorted pieces. Pastor Kurltree declared Jesus' ability to rebuild a person's life, that is, for a person who will rely on Jesus as Lord of his life."

"Did you see the picture of Jesus attached to the wall over Mister Cobblerman's work bench? I noticed it the day he sewed us together, the day Smarty Whippersnapper's dad bought us."

"I reckon Mister Cobblerman also believes in Jesus, just like Pastor Kurltree."

"Which means—Jesus acts as a senior partner to both Mister Cobblerman and Pastor Kurltree. If we ask Jesus to guide us, He can be our helper and senior partner just like theirs. Right?"

"We can't lose. I feel better already."

"Thank you, Jesus. We salute You as Lord, and the King of all Shoemakers."

6. PAPA'S ROCKING HORSE

(Revised September 19, 2013)
Clippity-clop, clippity-clop!

FIVE-YEAR-OLD JERI rode her granddad's white rocking horse with its black mane and tail over the hard-wood floor of her mother's living room. She bounced along, wide-eyed, happy, at times almost bucked off by her own energetic lurches.

She whinnied for her new companion, a full-bodied miniature Lipizzaner stallion with its shiny new coat of paint. Uncle Jeb had performed a magnificent renovation on her favorite playmate.

"Come wash your hands, Dear," her mother Sara, called from the kitchen. "I prepared a chicken-and-rice casserole with pumpkin pie and ice cream for our Christmas dinner."

"May I bring Jason, too?" Jeri inquired as she threw her right leg over the saddle horn and dismounted from Papa's cherished wooden horse.

"Yes. Lead him to the chair beside yours and tie his reins to one of its legs so he won't run away. We must be good to our animals and take care of them."

Throughout their Yuletide dinner, Jeri quizzed her mother about Papa. "Honey, my dad grew up in a family of wood carvers and cabinet makers. My dad loved to carve animals and birds." Sara beamed. "He learned the wood-carving skill from his father who made the rocking horse you named Jason."

"Did your dad give my horse a name?" she asked leaning forward with anticipation.

"I don't think so." With a shrug of her shoulders, she added, "He referred to his toy animal only as Horse."

Jeri petted Jason's mane, then looked up at her mother. "I think Papa's wooden horse should have a name."

"I agree, Sweetie." Sara hugged her daughter as the conversation about Horse and Papa continued. "I think it nice you gave our wooden friend the name Jason. It means he can act like a 'somebody' and hold his head high as you ride him."

Sara held her head high and raised a hand to emphasize the action as she spoke to reinforce the lesson for Jeri. "Everyone wants to be known by their own name."

"Momma," Jeri stopped eating her dessert, swallowed, and asked, "Did you ride Horse when you were my age?"

"No, Horse's left rear foot broke in a fall on the front steps of your grandpa's home when he rode too close to the edge of their porch. So, his dad placed Horse in their attic storeroom. The injured toy lay there, forgotten for years.

"But when Papa died last year, his brother Jeb thought you might like to ride Horse, like he and Grandpa rode him when they played together as kindergartners. Since he had been trained like the other members of Papa's family, he decided to repair Horse for your enjoyment."

A smile flashed across Jeri's face. "Momma, when will we see Uncle Jeb again? I want to thank him for giving me Jason."

"We may have dinner with Uncle Jeb and his family on Valentine's Day. They live a one-hour drive west of us. So, tomorrow we will write him a thank-you note and suggest dinner together, weather permitting."

With their dinner completed, Jeri continued her imaginary ventures in the living room with her new Christmas friend, Jason.

Clippity-clop, clippity-clop!

As Jeri's mother finished washing the dinner dishes, she heard—

Knock-knock.

333

She walked to her front door, wondered, *Who might come visit us on Christmas day?* A voice on the other side of the screen door said: "Mrs. Hausbricht, my name is Chaplain Jim Fanlucht, U.S. Army, on duty at Fort Sill, Oklahoma. Here is my picture ID and that of my assistant.

"Please excuse our interruption of your Christmas celebration. May we come in and speak with you a few minutes about the Afghanistan situation?"

Sara felt a dark cloud of uncertainty begin to suddenly envelope herself. "Yes, you may come in."

"First, let me confirm that you are Mrs. Sara Hausbricht."

"Yes, I am Sara Hausbricht." She felt a chill on her arms and a knot beginning to form in her stomach. Her mind questioned, *Has something happened to Dan?*

"May we sit down before stating our reason for coming today?"

"Surely. Come to the kitchen table with me. Is Dan injured?" Her slippers felt like lead weights, her legs wanted to tremble.

"I have some disturbing news about your husband." Chaplain Fanlucht spoke clearly and slowly, looking directly at Sara.

"I'm expecting a telephone call from him later this afternoon." Sara spoke rapidly, eyes wide open as she surveyed both men.

"I regret to inform you, your husband, Captain Daniel J. Hausbricht was killed two days ago while on patrol in Afghanistan."

Sara began to cry, ""Ooh Dan . . . my Dear . . . Dan."

"I have a letter for you from his commanding officer which describes the cause of his death. His body will arrive next Monday by plane and be accompanied by military escort to the Wessmir Funeral Home. Please contact them for his funeral arrangements, at which time we will send a military honor guard."

Sara sank to the floor, dazed, unable to speak, the remainder of the conversation a blur. After a few consoling words, Chaplain Fanlucht and his assistant determined Sara was not having a heart attack, but had become deeply overcome with grief.

They left quietly and closed the door behind themselves. Disbelieving the message and the matter-of-fact statement of her husband's death, shock overcame Sara. Her usual tempered emotions burst into anguished waves of uncontrollable tears.

Jeri, unaware of the visitors and her mother's distress from the unexpected conversation, continued to ride Jason. But hearing her mother's irrepressible groans, she shouted, "Momma, why are you crying?" Hurrying to the kitchen, she found her mother curled up like a ball in a corner near a window, weeping, and gasping for breath.

Sara reached for her daughter, clutched her tight, unable to say anything for several minutes. Her tears cascaded over Jeri's black hair.

"Momma . . . you sick? What's wrong?" Jeri asked, bewildered, knowing her mother had never acted this way before.

A half hour passed before Sara was able to straighten her legs on the floor, sit with her back against the wall, both arms wrapped around her precious daughter, holding her close.

Jeri knew she should not struggle to free herself, because something terrible had happened. Between outbursts of tears, Sara spoke with hesitation. "My Dear, your father will not come home this summer."

"Why, Momma?" Jeri didn't know how to react.

"Jesus has changed his assignment, and instead, made a home for Daddy with Him in Heaven."

"Did Daddy do something wrong?" Jeri felt confused, not knowing how to respond to her mother's distraught emotional outbursts. "Doesn't Jesus know I need Daddy here?"

"Something bad happened when Daddy went up a hill with his soldier friends. He cannot come home and be your father anymore." Sara tried to regain her composure and speak clearly to Jeri. "From now on, only you and I can be buddies."

"I don't understand. But, Momma, can Jason be a buddy with us?"

"Yes, my Dear, we shall include Jason as part of our family. Do you know why?"

"No."

"Jason will represent the Christmas spirit of Jesus' love for us, as he has for four generations in our family. And, Jason will symbolize our love for each other as we worship Jesus."

"I don't know what you mean, Momma, Jeri spoke hesitantly. "But may I go tell Jason, Daddy will not come home anymore?"

"Tell Jason we love Jesus, and we will see Jesus and Daddy—all our family, some day in Heaven."

"Okay, Momma." Jeri stood up, her tearful eyes downcast. Confused, she walked slowly toward the object of her understanding of Christmas, Papa's gift of love. Then, wrapping her arms around Jason's mane, she exclaimed, "I have something to tell you!"

Clippity-clop, clippity-clop!

7. PRESCRIPTION FOR THE MULLIGRUBS

[Describes acute colicky pain, depression, the blues, and mild to moderate stress]
(October 11, 2013)

CONUMER (THE PATIENT): Mr. Bob (Trombone player and friend of the Prescriber)

DIRECTIONS FOR USE:

NOTICE: FAILURE TO FOLLOW all directions with regularity may cause eye strain, disjointed thinking, tremors in toes, unusual speech patterns, failure to count from one to ten accurately, stomach cramps, itching in hands, throbbing headaches, and intermittent extreme nervousness.

First, remove wrapper.

Next, place only one tear-drop shaped chocolate inside your mouth at either side (your choice).

With a smile on your face, Savor slowly until completely melted, dissolved, and swallowed. For best results, administer after the noon meal.

However, in case of extreme stress, emotional trauma, or fainting spells associated with excessive frustration and anger over computer glitches, hang-ups, or its refusal to obey operator instructions, take one and only one additional tear-drop therapeutic comforter.

Like a pastry, it must be administered by the Missus, either only mid-morning, or only mid-afternoon, or only early evening, provided the Missus will agree to such a request after observing the Patient's unusual hypertensive behavior.

CAUTION: This drug is so potent, no refills will be recommended until after six months have elapsed. Consume at your own risk.

DIRECTIONS FOR STORAGE: The Missus should be in charge of the storage of this ailment reliever. She should secure this medicinal antidote in a secure, cool location, unknown to the recipient (e.g., hidden behind something in the refrigerator).

RECOMMENDED & ENDORSED BY:

Dr. CTC, Ph.D. (Fellow trombone horn blower)

NOTE: There is no known government approval, certification or endorsement, nor will there ever be, for either this remedy or the person writing this prescription.

8. MUSICAL ADJUDICATION COMMENTS

(December 10, 2012)

A S A FORMER TEEN Talent judge, I respectfully offer the following nuggets of observation and advice for Trombonist Mrs. "B."

For the high-brows among us, I would explain the word "adjudication" to mean a tasteful evaluation of each phrase performed in the ministry of this delightful ensemble which calls itself "New Horizons."

For the low-brows privileged to come and enjoy this spectacular presentation, the assessment will probably engender popcorn and cider toe-tapping reminders of childhood Christmas extravaganzas.

I however, have no idea how to differentiate between either perspective. Except the high-brow person may some-times lift their eyebrows in time with the tempo of the music.

The low-brow person may squint his eyes and comb his bushy eye brows to the side in order to see who is playing the melody at any particular moment during the presentation of each pleasing selection.

The following comments I must adamantly make clear, are for the sole perusal of Mrs. "B," musician *par excellence*, player this morning of that beautiful, shiny trombone, known historically by the German medieval term as a *sakbut*.

Criterion No. 1 – <u>Breath Support</u>: You performed in such a bold manner, it seemed to blow the tail feathers apart on three imitation cardinals sitting in a nearby Christmas tree. <u>Score</u>: 92 points (of 100 possible).

<u>Suggestion</u>: Next time when you play, focus your col-umn of hot air on the stand of music of the person immediately ahead of yourself and try to blow their music off their stand. They will most likely have memorized their part by the time you perform your next engagement. So, no problem.

Criterion No. 2 – <u>Tone</u>: Your horn resonated well as its fundamental frequency sounds gave buoyancy to the entire ensemble. The depth of quality of the sound by this group of musicians would be empty without your sonorous brass timbre. <u>Score</u>: 94 points (of 100 possible).

Suggestion: Try to blend with and match the harmonious intervals of others as much as possible. Don't overshadow the reeds. Be sure to enjoy every note you play. If those black specks start moving across the page or in a free-for-all, up and down motion, use a fly swatter and bang 'em still.

Criterion No. 3 – Intonation: Fortunately, your instrument has a slide assembly which enables *Der-Huff-und-Puffer* player to adjust the pitch slightly up or down, either sharp or flat, depending upon room temperature, nearby drafts, or the key of any composition being rendered by the group for the satisfaction of all persons in attendance, including players, listeners, and anyone passing by.

Score: As performed before lunchtime, 95 points (of 100 possible). Alternative points awarded for early brunch buddies, the before breakfast bash bunch—96 (of 97 possible, which includes a three point bonus. The golf guys call it a handicap.).

Suggestion: Eat a nutritious breakfast, but by-pass the frijoles.

Criterion No. 4 – Ensemble: This means everyone is expected to start and stop at certain designated times as written in their own particular part.

I suggest placing a moist, well-chewed piece of bubble gum, wrapped with a large Band Aid over and around the spit-valve apparatus in case of a leaky or sputtering water key.

I don't know which is worse—a wheezing instrument or a snoring old man, like myself, when such a nice ensemble like yours plays so tunefully, so congenially, so musically. **Score**: 98 points (of 100 possible).

Suggestion: Keep playing together regularly, irrespective of the lack of Christmas tree tinsel dangling from the brass bells of members horns and cotton-laced imitation snow drooping off the *apparati* of the low E keys and bells of the clarinets.

Criterion No. 5 – Phrasing: This evaluation element really implies that the melody shifts to a different instrument whenever a person's lips become tired of playing a bunch of melodic high notes or *arpeggiated* fast notes.

For we hapless individuals who most often play lots of "um-pa-pas," we must excel in counting 1-2-3-4 or 1-2-3 in groups of four or eight measures.

You've now learned that playing rests of whatever duration or tempo, is a downright rotten drag on the quality of your musicianship. **Score**: 89 points (of 100 possible).

Suggestion: Squirt some water spray on your inner slide tubing during a "l-o-n-g" rest in the music. This will result in an unexpected sound which will add good percussive accents to any syrupy or beloved melody.

Criterion No. 6 – General Effect: What a blast! Your repertoire performed this morning would wake the dead, cause them to praise the Lord, and result in a gigantic shout of Hallelujah. I sense revival in the air.

Could all you instrumentalists be an extension of the famed British Salvation Army Band? Or am I hearing the beginning of a renovated Benny Goodman or Tommy Dorsey Band?

At any rate, keep your "slush pump" working well. Your next "gig" may well be an engagement as a South Springfield, German Polka Band. **Score**: 110 points (of 100 possible).

Suggestion: A small group like "New Horizons" can be very versatile in both music and in dress. Will you be wearing lederhosen, bobby socks, or cowboy hats, next time we hear you play?

Thank you for inviting us, for performing so well, and for bringing a bit of the Old and New World Christian culture to us in an uplifting Christ-like manner.

God bless you and all your fellow *musikants*. and do have a most pleasant, peaceful, and joyful Merry Christmas! CTC.

9. A MANUAL FOR PLAYING "WASHERS"

(November 5, 2010)

TO: Sam
FROM: CTC
RE: This Treatise is an Exaggerated Spoof, albeit a Manual of Operations for Playing "Washers."

Dear Sam,

I WAS HAPPY to hear you are working on a doctorate at AGTS, and I've been reflecting about our conversation last Tuesday concerning 'washers.'

"I've enclosed a few questionable instructions about playing 'washers' in the hope of helping you relax a bit between those required times of reading tons of treatises and wheelbarrow loads of three and four pound scholarly books.

"Included also are four large and four small washers with this instructional manual for the purpose of occasionally diverting your mind from the multiplicity of ten-cylinder words and voluminous concepts requiring your constant ingestion of knowledgeable procedures, which will most certainly aid the increase of your problem-solving expertise.

"The game of 'washers' provides an uncomplicated diversion for tired doctoral candidates who regularly peruse the complex tomes of logistical Einsteinian principles assigned daily. (We doctors can concoct our own twelve-cylinder words.)

"'Washers' provides an outside recreational release from book-learning tension, but only on warm afternoons when the temperature ranges between 68 and 72^0F. Master's candidates are not allowed to participate in this heady pastime.

"Also, no women are allowed to develop the intricate skill of tossing a washer the required distance in order to drop it into a carefully dug hole, because they might end up with dirty hands, broken fingernails, or scratched digits.

"However, if they persist and will submit to wearing soft cotton gardening gloves, they may be permitted to participate with the condition they also are doctoral candidates or spouses of the main contenders.

"And if these women are allowed to participate, they should be given a handicap of one point at the beginning of each contest. (Giv'um a two point handicap when you know a special meal will soon be in preparation.) Your favorite graduate instructors—men or women, I might add, may 'toss' washers, too.

"The basic rules of the game will be determined by how tired the two competing doctoral candidates may be at the time of competition. When establishing the parameters of the contest, a starting line is first drawn in the sand, gravel, or dirt by the edge of a garden, driveway, walkway, or shoulder of a seldom-used road.

"Both contestants may feel somewhat revived by the fresh outside air, the invigorating atmosphere of birds singing nearby, and children squealing on playground swings. Perhaps the wafting smell of a barbecue supper in preparation may make their nostrils twitch in anticipation, and give additional relief from the tedium of an exhausting study day.

"However, I suggest a small hole, about three inches across and three inches deep be dug in the ground by using an old rusty soup spoon, at a distance of approximately seven feet from the line marker.

"A small garden spade no bigger than your hand is too big, too heavy, and too cumbersome. Conservation of energy is one of the goals of this event. All throws are tossed from the one starting line. The rusty soup spoon, of course, should be used to cover the hole at the end of any daily game, thereby saving dress shoes from scuffing or gym shoes from excessive wear.

"If both competitors feel quite haggard and non-plussed at game time, then I suggest a similar small hole be dug only six feet from the line marker. Stepping off the distance is perfectly acceptable.

"Measuring tapes are verboten; relative distances are the preferred norm. Preciseness in this duel destroys the relaxed atmosphere of reveling in this sedate and substitute physical activity.

"A participant may win the match when six or seven or even ten washers, as pre-determined by the tiredness of the scholars, have been successfully tossed into a carefully dug hole.

"'Washers' has been designated a substitute horseshoe sport, especially when horseshoe equipment and adequate space may not be readily available in order to play the real game of horseshoes.

"Please note, the 'washers' paraphernalia can be easily carried in the doctoral candidate's briefcase, computer bag, or even in his lunch pail without becoming offensive to the person's spouse.

"If the two players appear quite tired from the heady interaction of recent interrogative and expository classroom dialogues, much less late-hour library snoozing, they may switch equipment from the large washers to the smaller thumb-and-first-finger sized washers in order to relieve pent up emotions or aching computer hand-back-arm muscle tension.

"During your participation in this diversionary under-taking, I suggest you consider naming one washer 'faith' and the other 'hope.' The size of the hole would need to be enlarged slightly should you decide to toss a third washer 'love.' Other names may be assigned as desired. I think the spiritual applications may be endless in an accompanying dialogue between partners in this esoteric game.

"At any rate, names of instructors should not be used for either washer during this procedure and game time of renewing spiritual awareness and physical energy. (If desired, you may fashion your own guidelines.)

"Sam, I learned the intricacies of playing 'washers' at the University of Iowa in 1964 while working on my doctorate. My neighbor, also a doctoral candidate, instructed me one summer afternoon in the joy of playing this stress-relieving game.

"Since we bested the other guys in a horseshoe tournament at the North Dakota Campground, I believe it was the summer of 1986 when you and Gordon were the speakers, and since you are now working on a doctoral program, I thought you might enjoy this inspirational leisure pursuit, albeit humorous description, of a seldom practiced activity of some doctoral candidates journeying through the avenues of higher learning.

"God bless, and God speed in your study. With warm regards,

Charles."

10. A SPECIAL DISH CRASHED TO THE FLOOR!

(January 10, 2015)

MILDRED WALKED INTO her kitchen and started to prepare their supper. As she opened the cabinet door over the left end of her counter, the special china dish, a gift from her grandmother, fell out and crashed on the floor, breaking into several unrepairable pieces.

Sparky, her pet skunk, jumped out of the cupboard, streaked high over Mildred's head, and hit the wood floor, running as if jet propelled. He scrambled through his small two-way, entry-exit in the back door of the workroom adjacent to the kitchen.

A flying shard of the once precious dish hit the panel of his escape hatch as his bushy tail disappeared. "You rascal,"

Aunt Mil screamed, eyes ablaze, "How in heaven's name did you manage to find a way inside my dish cabinet?

"I'll skin you alive next time I see you inside my house." Through narrowed eyelids, sixty-seven-year-old Mildred jabbed her eight-inch hunting knife into the end of her wood countertop.

"That's the thanks I get for befriending the little tyke. I wish Cousin Jeb had killed him, too. Why did he run out of ammo immediately after he shot the squirt's mother and his siblings?"

Mildred tapped her forehead with a doubled-up fist: *I know I should have listened to my neighbor and left him for the rats. But I felt sorry for the little guy. He meowed with hunger, I knew he would make a fine pet.*

"But this time, Sparky, you went too far in all your playful capers. No more pretending to mark your territory by wetting on my recliner. No more eating an egg in the chicken coop when I'm gathering eggs in the hen house.

"Wait a minute, my ten-year-old niece, Honeybell, played hide and seek with you this morning around the living room. Perhaps, I should ask her if she knows how you somehow crawled inside my dish cabinet," *and why you were so anxious to depart the premises. Umm, yes, she might be able to explain how you—you, you mischievous stinker hid in my cupboard.*

Honeybell came, as usual, the next morning about ten o'clock to visit with her Aunt Mildred and to play with Sparky.

Aunt Mil bided her time about asking pointed questions. She continued to weed her garden as they greeted each other and talked about how big the carrots, onions and radishes grew during the last week.

Somewhat later, Aunt Mil asked Honeybell, "Oh, by the way, Bell babe, tell me how you and Sparky play tag or hide-n-seek in the house, while I'm out here cultivating my strawberries or watering my pumpkins. I'm interested in your games."

Honeybell, detected the bit of urgency of the mild, but pointed question. Little Bell thought quickly: *Had Sparky done something wrong? Did he break something? Did he go to the bathroom in the wrong place" Was Sparky sick?*

Mildred spoke again, composure almost smooth, "Yesterday, I went to my kitchen to prepare the evening meal. As I opened a cupboard door to take out dishes, Sparky came out causing a dish to crash on the floor. He literally flew out of the cabinet and high-tailed his exit out of his little two-way door through my wash room.

"Come Bell, let's sit down on this bench by the water pipe. Could you explain why Sparky sat on my dishes in a closed cabinet for such a long time?"

"Yes, Auntie," Bell laughed, "I placed him there when we played hid-n-seek yesterday. You see, when I hide, he smells me, wherever I may hide. He always finds me.

"I thought he could push the door open with his paw and come find me. I'm sorry, Auntie Mil, please forgive me." Bell's face lost its pink glow. "Guess I acted awful bad. I promise I won't do it again."

Aunt Mil remained quiet for a few moments, letting the realization of the error sink deep into her niece's consciousness.

"Honeybell, dear, I know you did not mean to do a shameful action. I forgive you, I really do. But it makes me realize that Sparky is no longer a two-week old baby skunk that needs help in order to survive. I think he must be about one year old now. We must think of his future. He can't live with me forever.

"Bell babe, this afternoon I will return him to the wooded area, some five miles from here, where I found him."

"No, Auntie, please don't do it. He's my best friend. Sparky wouldn't know what to do or how to act out in the wild!"

"My dear, you play with Sparky this morning. After lunch, You and I will take him to the woods where he can live out his life with his own kind."

"Oh, Auntie Mil, please, no—no!"

—TO BE CONTINUED—

11. AUNT BERTHA'S CHESS STRATEGY

(March 27, 2015)

THESE DAYS I SIT in my wheelchair at this retirement complex and make an attempt at civility. At age 95, people think the good life passed by me in yesteryear. However, I know better.

"Take note, Hank. I've ask the Lord to give me 120 years on earth, should He tarry. Or, if He decides to catch up the whole batch of us in the air one of these tumultuous days, I'm ready.

"You see, Hank, my boy – yes, I know you're 71 years old. Jesus thinks like my Filipino friends. They make room in their homes for overnight guests, regardless of how many relatives may live in their modest accommodations. It's the culture!

"Similarly, my buddy, the Lord feels the same way about the body of Christ. I hear Him reiterate daily as I read His Word: 'Come join Me. You're welcome in My house. Plan to live with Me for eternity. I've plenty of room for you in My heavenly home. My written Word explains the way. Come! The Holy Spirit will help make you comfortable!'

"Sonny, I believe His call goes out to little ones, youngsters, moms and dads, grandmas and grandpas, those whose lives likely slipped into the gutter, and to those persons riding on a false high.

"It's true, my young friend, I don't have many visitors these days. Most of my friends and acquaintances passed on earlier to glory-land. The individuals I interact with these days walk right into my parlor unannounced.

"These staff members mean well. But some look at me as just part of their job to perform. Others see me as a teacher or comforter for their personal situations.

"For example, Red, a nurse will stride into my room, three times each day. I must say, she arrives quite forcefully and informs me: 'Take this pill ("Most capsules look as big as your thumb nail.") . . . Swallow this pasty liquid ("She calls it tasty tapioca.") . . . Eat this banana' ("You need these vitamins bound up in your fruit.").

"At any time, day or evening, a male attendant my come barging into my room. He often interrupts my Bible reading. His story carries the same excuse: 'The chief said, the chief told me. The chief sent me to mop your floor and vacuum the rugs. Gotta move you out of your room into the corridor for a little while.'

"Mister Hank, that means several minutes, even an hour or more of displacement from my room. Humph! I sit out there in a cool draft, while his equipment makes loud, piercing noises.

"Fortunately, I can move my arm quick enough to grab my Bible from the night stand before he whisks me out of my room. I find not many residents read their Bibles.

"When I attempt a polite Bible discussion with any of my neighbors, even members of the staff, few of them know what I'm talking about. They could care less.

"For instance, several persons may know a whale swallowed Jonah (excuse me, 'a big fish' for you purists). But they can't tell me any details of God's call on Jonah's life.

"Oh, my dear, so many people still need Jesus in their lives and marriages. My prayer list overflows with names of people for whom I feel compelled to intercede. It's hard work. Nevertheless, I persevere each day by the strength and guidance of the Holy Spirit.

"But let me tell you a secret. At times, I compromise. I will play bingo with a resident, if he or she will promise to come to the activities room with me for a Bible study. My method works quite well.

"However, my friend, I prefer to relax by playing a timed game of chess with an individual who knows the game. By the way, sir, how about a quick game of chess this afternoon? You know, it's quite a restful activity. For me, it reduces the stress of the day. Say, with two hours yet before dinner, we might play best two-out-of-three."

"Okay, Auntie. But I won't let you win this time. Yet, I will give you the privilege of moving first."

"Thank you, you're a gentleman. As my nephew, I'm glad to see your good manners."

. . . "Well, Auntie, we each won a game. I believe I shall win game three today."

"Don't count your eggs before the hens lay them, you rascal. This M n' M I just ate supercharged my battery. Watch out where you move those castles and bishops. I feel I can end this challenge in six, maybe eight moves."

"Oops, wrong move with that knight. Sorry, I wasn't thinking. You caught me napping."

"Son, place those dead pieces by the side of the board. Please don't hold them in your hand. You know I can't see as well as I think. I want to visually account for all pieces – on the board and off the board."

"Okay, Aunt Bertha. I do that ruse with the youngsters that play with me. It upsets their concentration on the game."

"Well, well, well!" Can it be? I see a king, a castle, a rook, and a knight left for each of us. Hank, don't give me the game. I must work for it."

"No way, Auntie. For once, I would enjoy beating you, fair and square, two out of three games. Aah, you're not going to give me this game and purposefully lose?"

RING, RING.

"Oh, that blasted dinner bell. Hank, we must stop. If I don't eat regularly, my hypoglycemia will kick in, low blood sugar, you know."

"Okay, I concede. Your pieces set in a better position than mine. I don't like to admit it, but you're still the champ chess player. Perhaps, Aunt Bertha, if Jesus would come now and snatch us up to His heavenly home, we needn't worry about this game interruption at a crucial moment by a mealtime bell."

"Mister H, my good man, you're right. We'll leave the chess game here for others to fuss over. I believe the Lord will give us more important projects up there to accomplish for His glory."

AUTHOR'S BIOGRAPHY

REVEREND CHARLES T. CLAUSER ministered as an Assembly of God missionary, teacher and administrator for over 25 years in the Philippines. Earlier, he served stateside for 20 years as a music teacher and college administrator.

In 1974, Dr. Clauser joined the faculty of Trinity Bible Institute (now College), Ellendale, North Dakota and became chairman of the music department in 1976. Two years later, he began serving as activing academic dean.

Arriving in the Philippines in 1982, Charles taught at the Far East Advanced School of Theology (now Asia Pacific Theological Seminary) and at Bethel Bible College located on the same campus in Metro Manila.

Charles and Mary Clauser trained Christian workers and lay people, conducted short-term seminars for pastors, and ministered at district meetings. They also taught two- and three-week block sessions as adjunct faculty at various Bible schools in the Philippines.

Dr. Clauser taught in the Chinese Servant Leadership Institute at United Bethel Church in Manila. He served 17 years on the board of the Bible Institute for the Deaf in Metro Manila.

During their last term in the Philippines, Rev. Clauser assisted as OIC at the King's Garden Children Home located in Upper Sabatan, Orion, Bataan, Philippines. This ministry included upgrading facilities and coordinating two construction projects at the Home.

Charles T. Clauser

Dr. Clauser self-published a book of memoirs entitled *Family and Friends, Together Forever* (2011). Two additional books are in the process of completion. He has been a member of the Ozarks Chapter of the American Christian Writers for six years and served as its writing contest chairperson for five of those years.

The Clausers retired to Maranatha Village in Springfield, Missouri in May 2004. Their present ministry includes writing, music and visitation at Maranatha Village, and in area hospitals.

www.ingramcontent.com/pod-product-compliance
Lightning Source LLC
La Vergne TN
LVHW011216080426
835509LV00005B/155